Contents

Job-Hunting on the Internet

the parachute library

Job-Hunting
on the Internet

FOURTH EDITION

Richard Nelson Bolles
and
Mark Emery Bolles

TEN SPEED PRESS
Berkeley | Toronto

Ten Speed Press
Box 7123
Berkeley, California 94707
www.tenspeed.com

Distributed in Australia by Simon and Schuster Australia, in Canada by Ten Speed Press Canada, in New Zealand by Southern Publishers Group, in South Africa by Real Books, and in the United Kingdom and Europe by Airlift Book Company.

Cover design by Betsy Stromberg
Text design by Star Type, Berkeley

Library of Congress Cataloging-in-Publication Data
Bolles, Richard Nelson.
    Job-hunting on the Internet / Richard Nelson Bolles and
    Mark Emery Bolles. — 4th ed.
        p.   cm.
    Summary: "A companion book to *What Color Is Your Parachute?*
    to teach readers how to use the Internet in the job hunt" —
    Provided by publisher.
        Includes bibliographical references and index.
        ISBN-10: 1-58008-652-7 (pbk.)
        ISBN-13: 978-1-58008-652-3 (pbk.)
    1. Job hunting — United States — Computer network resources.
    2. Web sites — United States — Directories. I. Bolles, Mark Emery,
    1955–   II. Title.
HF5382.75.U6B65 2005
025.06'65014 — dc21   2005003418

Printed in the United States of America
First printing, 2005

1 2 3 4 5 6 7 8 9 10 — 09 08 07 06 05

Introduction

REVOLUTIONARY TIMES

It is difficult to turn on the television or read a newspaper these days without running into some reference to our new "data society," or the "Internet revolution." Do you feel like a revolutionary? I sure don't, and yet I can't imagine what life would be like without this machine that adorns—well, dominates—my desk (and at times my life) and its ability to instantly reach out to millions of others like it around the globe.

The world is going through a profound change, no less than the one caused by the printing press back in the fifteenth century. It is interesting to note that movable type had been around for some hundreds of years before Gutenberg, but it was the availability of inexpensive paper that allowed the printing press to find its power. Similarly, the core of the Internet can be traced back to the primitive networks of poles and wire that were strung with the invention of the telegraph in the mid-nineteenth century, converted and improved for telephone use in the twentieth century, and yet again with fiber optics, satellites, and transistor switching for the twenty-first.

But like paper for the press, it is the ubiquity of the inexpensive personal computer that has brought the Internet its real power and reach. Today, the amount of information exchanged in a single minute is more than Samuel Morse or Alexander Graham Bell could have read, telegraphed, or spoken in their entire lives. As with paper and the printing press, the Internet and the personal computer have transformed the world economy, changed the way that knowledge is shared and gathered, accelerated the pace of human invention, and now serve as a powerful force for literacy.

And the phenomenon continues to accelerate at amazing speed. Internet usage has increased by 100 percent in the last four years. Out of around 294 million people in the United States, 207 million of them have directly used the Internet at one time or another—that's over 70 percent of the population. In the same period, Net usage in Central America increased by over 300 percent; in some countries, such as Guam, the figure is over 800 percent. In many countries, including Japan, Germany, the United Kingdom, Italy, and Australia, more than half of the population uses the Internet directly.

No matter how we may think of ourselves, whether we feel like revolutionaries or not, you and I are deeply involved in this profound world change. A hundred years from now, when school children are learning about the people who were part of the world when it changed so quickly and so completely, it will be *us* that they are talking about.

THE INTERNET AND JOB-HUNTING

And in this changed world, where the economy, and the world of work, have shifted so dramatically and in such a short time, it is inevitable that even the way that we *find* our work has changed as well. In the United States, on any day, more than four million people are using the Internet to look for work. A 2002 survey report noted that more than fifty-two million Americans had used the Internet in some capacity to search for jobs. Of those who were unemployed, over half had Internet access, and at least 10 percent of those were searching on the Net *daily*. This is revolution indeed.

But not everyone who looks for work using the Internet is successful; in many ways, we are still at the beginning of this revolution. So far, the Net has *not* proved to be a magic wand; it has not changed the essential nature of job-hunting. When using the Internet for this purpose, most people treat it as if it were a high-tech want-ad section of the newspaper, but this is not the Internet's strength. If that's the way you choose to use the Net for *your* job hunt, then your chances of finding a job with it are less than 10 percent, which is pretty bad.

Instead, you should view the Internet as a tool, just like any other. You need to learn how best to wield this tool, and then use

it as just one of many such tools at your disposal, in an overall *strategy* for your job hunt. The book you now hold was written to teach you how to use this tool, and how to implement the Internet part of your job-hunting strategy efficiently.

THE PARACHUTE SERIES

Job-Hunting on the Internet is part of Ten Speed Press's Parachute job-hunting series. *What Color Is Your Parachute?* is the best-selling job-hunting book of all time, with more than eight million copies in print and rising. The reason that *Parachute* is so popular is simple: it is because it works. The ideas in *Parachute* have been well tested over three decades, and have helped *millions* of people find work—and not just any work, but work that they love to do. Your job-hunt will be most successful, on the Internet and off, if you have a strategy that follows the three central themes of *Parachute,* which can be summed up as WHAT, WHERE, and HOW:

- Discover *what* your best and most enjoyable skills are.

- Choose *where* you want to use these skills, by identifying the fields of interest, geographical area, and the working conditions in which you will use them.

- Decide *how* you will go about finding this job, by identifying the organizations that interest you most and finding the person there with the power to hire.

The Internet can be terrific at helping you implement such a strategy. Used well, it will increase your chances of job-hunting success considerably. As an important member of the *Parachute* series, this book shows you how you can use the Internet to get you as quickly as possible to work, doing the kind of work you most like to do.

WHEN LESS IS MORE

The dot-com crash of a few years ago taught us a number of important lessons; in my mind, two stand out. The first is: *don't give your life savings to a bunch of twenty-three year olds* (which seems pretty obvious when you think about it, but I could be wrong). The second is: *people don't want a hundred choices for everything.* How many grocery stores do you shop at? How many dry cleaners do you go to? How many different routes do you take on your way to work? People want to have a reasonable number of options to choose from, but they don't want to be overwhelmed by options, by a tyranny of choice. If it was nothing else, the dot-com bust was human nature raising its voice, saying that people don't want so many different companies, each doing the exact same thing.

We can apply the same principle to books about the Internet. You may have noticed that many books about the Net are nothing but a long list of website addresses, essentially leaving to *you* the work of figuring out which ones will work best. With an estimated forty thousand job-related sites on the Internet, listing even 10 percent of these would be useless to you. You don't want to know every job site available; you want to know which ones will be most helpful to you in your job-hunt.

So, rather than being a complete index of Internet job-hunting sites, this book is a collection of carefully chosen ones, sites that I

think will help you find the work you want, quickly and efficiently. If I didn't think that a site would be helpful, or if there were many others better in its category, then that site was not listed in the book. Only the best (in my opinion) made it in.

And, from among these chosen few, I have further narrowed the field by selecting those that I think are *especially* good, and I have called them Parachute Picks, with a Parachute symbol alongside their listing, thus:

This means that for job-hunting purposes, this is one of the best sites on the Web, in the category it is listed in.

And with the sites that I *have* listed, I try to be honest about what they have to offer and what they don't. In some cases, I'll highly recommend a site for doing *this* thing but not for doing *that.* You need to know the difference, if you're going to find the work that you want to do as quickly as possible, using the Internet.

INTERNET ACCESS

Naturally, to use this book effectively, you will need a computer with Internet access. If you don't have one, at home or at work, (or have a friend who will let you use theirs), you can usually find one that you can rent for a fee, or sometimes use for free, by going to any of the following:

- One of the increasingly popular commercial *Internet cafes.* These are known by different names around the world— Net cafes, cybercafes, public Internet access points and kiosks—a list of 6,318 of them in over 167 countries (as of 6/27/04) can be found at *The Cybercafe Search Engine* at www.cybercaptive.com. A similar list of some 4,200 Internet cafes in 140 countries can be found at www.cybercafes.com.

- Your local public library (many librarians will take the trouble to show you how to use a computer, if it's all new to you).

- Your local state or government employment center.

- Internet kiosks in all kinds of places: airports, airplanes, hotels, cruise ships, freeway rest stops, bookstores, stationery stores, coffee shops, and local print shops, including places like McDonalds, Starbucks, and FedEx Kinko's.

If you do have your own computer and it's portable, you don't necessarily need to have Internet access at home; wireless access hot spots are being created, increasingly, all around the globe, from burger joints to baseball stadiums. Some 11,700 are listed at:

`www.hotspot-locations.com,`
`www.wi-fihotspotlist.com,`
`www.wi-fizone.org,` or
`www.wififreespot.com.`

FOR-FEE SITES $$

The Internet's popularity is due, in great part, to the fact that it is essentially free. Most attempts to turn the Internet into a fee-for-service business—at least in the job-hunting world—have met with failure, and you will find that most websites do not charge for access. But there are exceptions, occasionally even worthy ones, and as you go about your job-hunt on the Internet, you will find some sites that are fee-driven, generally involving subscriptions allowing access to specific data for a certain length of time. As always when on the Net, be careful reaching for your credit card: security is no small issue.

And as for whether you should spend money at all . . . don't let desperation in your job-hunt make "buy/don't buy" decisions for you. I have identified fee-for-service sites in this book with dollar signs thus: $$, though many of these fee-for-service sites will allow you free access for a certain trial period.

USING THIS BOOK

Throughout this book, I've listed the URLs, or addresses, of the various websites under discussion. Not only is it a pain to type all of these URLs into a Web browser, but it is easy to make mistakes.

To solve this problem, you may go to the Job-Hunter's Bible website at

www.jobhuntersbible.com,

where you will find a (regularly updated) collection of all of the hyperlinks in this book. You can operate on them from the JHB site, download the link pages to your computer, or import the links into your Favorites or Bookmarks for easy use. That way, you need only click on the site you want, avoiding the laborious typing of URLs.

Also at the Job-Hunter's Bible site, you will find articles and recent information about the Internet as it applies to the job-hunt. By using the site as your entry door to the Internet during your job-hunt, you will have tremendous resources right at your fingertips.

And, if you find yourself stuck, or feeling temporarily beaten by our society's Neanderthal job-hunting system, Job-Hunter's Bible offers answers by email to your job-hunting questions. This unique service is also free.

BOOK UPDATES

Writing a book about the Internet is like taking a snapshot of the weather: initially accurate but unlikely to be so for long. The Net is constantly changing; links are broken, pages move, and as Internet expert Mary-Ellen Mort says, Web addresses turn bad faster than an egg salad. If you find a URL that doesn't work, either in this book or at the Job-Hunter's Bible website, please let us know immediately, at `jobhunter@wt.net`.

In spite of my spending more time than I want to think about on the Internet, I'm certain there are a lot of good sites about which I know nothing—at least, not yet. If you, as a job-hunter, find a site that was particularly useful to you in your job-hunt, and you therefore think it should be listed in the next edition of this book, please let me know, again by emailing me at `jobhunter@wt.net`. And if you operate a site that you think would be helpful to other readers (and isn't a resume distribution service or other scheme that you know runs counter to the central ideas in *Parachute*), please let me know, at the same address.

CHAPTER ONE

Job-Hunting and the Internet

Back in 1985, the late John Crystal used to describe the ridiculousness of our traditional job-hunting "system." A job-hunter, he said, would be walking down a street, despairing of ever finding the work he wanted, and brushing past him, with a hurried "Excuse me," would be an employer who was hunting desperately for exactly that man or woman with exactly those talents and experience. But that would be the last they would ever see of each other. Our job-hunting "system" had not yet come up with any good way for them to ever find each other, and instead, they had passed like ships in the night.

As people have, over the years, cast about for solutions to this problem, they have found that one of the most powerful tools now available is the Internet, and in particular, that part of the Internet known as the *World Wide Web*.

The Web—and the Internet in general—is growing at an astonishing rate. In fact, while radio took thirty-eight years to gain fifty million listeners, and television took thirteen years to gain that number of viewers, the Internet, as we currently know it, took just four years to gain that number of users. And now, in the United States alone, more than 207 million adults—over 70 percent of the population—have Internet access at home or at work. Worldwide, the figure is more than 785 million, which represents an increase, in the last four years, of 118 percent.

1

The U.S. Department of Commerce has said that with the Internet's tremendous growth (which shows no signs of abating), the amount of information being processed over the Internet is doubling every hundred days. Some of that information is, of course, devoted to job-hunting—and it is increasing along with all the rest. And more and more people flocking to the Internet means more and more job-hunters gaining access. A recent report shows that in one month alone—April of 2003—more than seventeen million people logged on to career sites on the Internet.

JOB-HUNTING

When the time comes to go job-hunting, you basically have two choices about the type of job-hunt you will perform: the traditional job-hunt, or the more targeted, creative (some say "life-changing") job-hunt.

The traditional job-hunt is essentially a matching game. You compare a list of skills you have against a list of skills an employer needs, and if the two match closely enough, you apply for the position. If the prospective employer agrees that you are a close match to what they want, then you'll be hired. Often, there may be no actual list of skills; you may summarize the skills under a job title, like "carpenter" or "systems analyst." But it's still the same thing; you have a certain view of what you can do and are looking for a pigeonhole into which you can file yourself, for the sake of employment.

The creative job-hunt is more complex, and takes more work, but it will usually reward you with more job satisfaction, higher salary, and greater personal fulfillment. This type of job-hunt has eight simple rules:

- Know your best and most enjoyable skills. These skills are transferable, from one occupation to another. You are not just your job title.
- Know what kind of work you want to do, what field you would most enjoy working in.
- Talk to people who are doing the work you want to do in that field. Find out how they like the work and how they found their job.

- Do some research, then, in your chosen geographical area, on those organizations that interest you, to find out what they do and what kinds of problems/challenges they or their industry are wrestling with.

- Then identify and seek out the person who actually has the power to hire you at each organization, for the job you want; use your personal contacts—everyone you know—to get in to see him or her.

- Show this person with the power to hire you how you can help them with their problems/needs/challenges and how you would stand out as "one employee in a hundred."

- Don't take turndown or rejection personally. Remember, there are two kinds of employers out there: those who will be bothered by your handicaps—age, background, inexperience, or whatever they are—and those who won't be, and will hire you, so long as you can do the job. If the first kind of employer rejects you, keep persevering, until you find the second.

- In all of this, cut no corners, take no shortcuts.

Obviously, this type of job-hunt requires you to carefully inventory your skills, particularly the ones you most enjoy using, so that you know what it is you want to be doing with half of your waking life; define in what field of endeavor and under what conditions, you want to use these skills; and research those organizations you want to work for, who are in need of the skills you possess. Sometimes that organization may not have an actual job opening, but if you identify the person in that organization with the power to hire, and demonstrate to them that you have the skills to solve their problems, then they will often create a position for you.

The job-hunt that you need to perform right now may be somewhere in between these two types, as I have described them. As a job-hunter, you must assess your current situation, make some decisions on how you will go about your job-hunt, and come up with a strategy, a plan, for how you are going to approach this challenge in your life. And the Internet can be extremely helpful, both in helping you come up with a job-hunting strategy, and in implementing it, regardless of the kind of job-hunt you decide to pursue.

Of course, *this* book alone is not meant to teach you how to come up with such a strategy. For that, you should pick up a recent copy of *What Color Is Your Parachute?* (I say "recent," because it is updated every year, as the world changes) and read it cover to cover, at least once. When you have done that, you should know enough to be able to use this book more effectively to formulate and implement the Internet portion of your job-hunting strategy.

THE INTERNET

What is the Internet to the job-hunter? I think the most useful answer is to say that the Internet is a place where a job-hunter can perform certain tasks, and when you break it down this way, the Internet becomes five places to the job-hunter:

- A place where you can get some skills testing, career counseling, and job-hunting advice.

- A place to do research, to find out information about fields, occupations, jobs, companies, cities, geographical areas, salaries, and so on.

- A place to make contacts and network with people, who can help you find information, or suggest referrals, or help you get in for an interview at a particular place.

- A place where you can post your own resume, for the benefit of employers who are looking to fill vacancies.

- A place for you to search for vacancies listed by employers (often called "want ads," "job postings," or "job listings").

Testing, Counseling, and Advice

The Internet is a place where you can get some skills testing, career counseling, and job-hunting advice.

If you are unsure about certain aspects of your job-hunt— what your skills are, how to overcome certain obstacles, or map out a job-hunting strategy—you'll find that the Internet offers a variety of resources to help you bring these matters into clearer focus. This may involve taking some tests, to see what skills you have and prefer to use in your work. Or, you can read some of the thousands of online articles, Usenet postings, and Web advice columns on careers, or perhaps subscribe to some job-hunting newsletters to help you get a better idea of how to go about your job-hunt. And if you are really stuck, you might even get some one-on-one counseling from a job-hunting expert on your particular situation. The Internet can help you with all of these. On the downside, this is the one area of your job-hunt where using the Internet is most likely to cost you money, due to various fees, but you can still find most of these services for free, as well, if you know where to look for them.

Research

The Internet is a place to do research, to find out information about fields, occupations, jobs, companies, cities, geographical areas, salaries, and so on.

If I had to pick the one category that the Internet does best, out of the five I have listed, then this would be it. And research is also the most important job-hunting Internet skill for you to master. Why is this? Because it is through research that you will be able to find the fields where your skills can best be used; the types of companies in those fields; and from there, the specific companies, in the geographical area where you want to work, that might hire you.

Early on, most companies who hired employees through the Internet found most of these people through the job boards. Far fewer came through the companies' own websites—no doubt because so few companies even *had* a website. But that trend has now shifted: a 2003 study found that of those companies that hired people using the Internet, 59 percent of their Net-hired employees were found through the companies' own websites. The next most successful method—hiring through one of the large job boards—was used only 14 percent of the time.

This is significant to you as a job-hunter, for if potential employers are depending less on the job boards and more on company websites, so must you. You must learn to do the research necessary to find the companies you are interested in working for and who might, in turn, be interested in you. But note the benefits: if you do this research properly, your chances of getting hired are four times greater than if you just post your resume on one of the job boards.

The skills you learn while doing this research will be valuable after your job-hunt, as well. These days, Internet skills are becoming more and more important in an ever-growing number of jobs. If an employer has to make a choice between two people, for hiring or for promotion, and one has better Internet research skills, who do you think will most likely be chosen?

Contacts
The Internet is a place to network with people who can help you find information, or suggest referrals, or help you get in for an interview at a particular place.

In another 2003 study, the figures for successful job-seekers broke down this way: 2 percent found their jobs through employment agencies, up to 7 percent directly through the Internet, 9 percent through "walk-ins," 16 percent through newspaper ads, and 61 percent through personal contacts and networking. One more time: *61 percent of job-seekers found their jobs through personal contacts.* So let's see . . . if you had a 7 percent chance of finding a job by posting your resume online, and a 61 percent chance of finding a job by going through your contacts, which would you choose?

Other studies bear this out, and, unusual in the world of statisticians, the results are remarkably consistent for both employer

and job-hunter. *Employers* fill most of their vacancies through the recommendations of people they know or through people who already work for them. *Job-hunters* find that using contacts is the most successful single method of finding employment (though I don't want you to get the impression that I advocate any *single* method of job-hunting—just the opposite). Luckily for both, this is an area where the Internet has a number of resources to offer.

Job Postings and Resume Postings

The Internet is a place for you to search for vacancies listed by employers (often called "want ads," "job postings," or "job listings"), and the Internet is a place where you can post your own resume for the benefit of employers who are looking to fill vacancies.

This is what most people think of when you talk about online job-hunting: look through the (thousands of) job postings online, where the perfect job is already waiting for you. Or post your resume on the job boards, and you'll get at least five emails tomorrow with jobs that match you perfectly, and you'll barely have to lift a finger.

So . . . if it works so great, why did you buy this book? Or maybe you've already found out that, in fact, this is the one part of the job-hunt where the performance of the Internet is poorest. The data varies, and is not particularly recent, but studies show that only between 4 and 7 percent of people find their jobs this way. The percentage is higher in certain fields than in others. I don't think anyone would be surprised to learn that the chances of being hired through an Internet job board are better for a computer programmer than they are for a plumber. But there it is.

There are, however, things you can do to make this part of the Internet more effective during your job-hunt. As well, there are specialized job boards and places you can go that cater to certain specialties and trades—an example might be a job board for, say, plumbers. Like the one at `www.mepatwork.com`.

JOB-HUNTING AND THE INTERNET

The Net is one tool, one approach, one method, that you may use when job-hunting. But it is not—and shouldn't be—the only way you go about your job-hunt. Too often, people think that all they have to do is post their resume online, and they will automatically have ten job offers sitting in their in-box when they check their email the next morning. Occasionally, that does happen; occasionally, people win the lottery, too. But most people *don't* win the lottery . . . and that isn't a problem, as long as when you buy your lottery ticket, you don't have an unrealistic expectation of winning.

Job-hunting is hard enough as it is. If your expectation is that the Internet is going to fix all of your woes, and the inevitable letdown occurs, then you are going to be just a little more disappointed, a little more depressed, and a little less hopeful. It's an erosion process. Too much of it can be paralyzing, when activity and movement are called for.

So let's put your expectations in the proper place. Try some of these statistics on for size:

- In a study of three thousand Internet-using job-hunters, only 4 percent got their jobs solely through their online efforts.

- In another study, it was found that only 8 percent of employers' new hires were from the Internet.

- And in yet another study, this from the University of Washington, unemployed people in the study group were found to be 3 percent more likely to have found a job if they used the Internet. Two years later, the figure had changed: the unemployed were found to be 3 percent *less* likely to have found a job if they used the Internet.

Yikes. That is just *awful.* But now, let's take a closer look at these statistics. To start with, all of the studies done to date have asked the wrong questions. They ask, "Did you use the Internet to find a job? Did it work?" At the time these studies were done, the number of people who *only* used the Internet to find a job were successful about 4 percent of the time.

But that's not the right way to use the Internet. For example, you can purchase things over the Net, but you don't buy *everything* there; that would be silly. It's great for buying books or ordering some discount gifts or maybe getting something through eBay. But most people don't buy their groceries on the Net, or run to their computer instead of the hardware store when they need a nail. You *can* use the Net for many things (even grocery shopping), but it isn't the *best* solution for everything.

So, when doing a survey on the Internet's job-hunting effectiveness, the *right* questions would be, "Did you use the Internet as part of an overall strategy for finding a job?" and "Did this help you get a job?" The response to *those* questions would probably reveal a success rate as great as any other job-hunting method. I'll say it again: the Net is not meant to stand alone; it is *one* tool in your job-hunting arsenal. It is not meant to be your *only* tool.

I personally believe that the statistics paint a picture that is much poorer than the actual reality. For example, much of the data, and most of the studies done concerning the Internet and job-hunting are from the period 1996 through 2000. I have found virtually no government data, and very little private data, from 2003 to the present. What data I have found is marginally more encouraging. For example, in a report from July 2004, Nielson/Net Ratings reported that traffic to Internet career sites had jumped 30 percent in the last year, with almost 27.2 million people visiting. Nearly 18 percent of all people with Internet access had visited a career site during this period, making job-hunting one of the major uses of the Internet—*now.* The Nielson/Net

Ratings report also shows a lot of repeat visits and loyalty to certain career sites. People don't normally continue to do what doesn't work, so I find that encouraging as well.

Bear in mind that the underlying technology, and the Internet's very structure, make it correct itself very quickly. The whole dot-com bust taught us that if something isn't working, this technology allows for very rapid change. Over time, people are learning what the Internet does well, and what it does not. Clearly, with its tremendous capacity to inform and bring people together, job-hunting is something that the Net *can* do well, if it is used properly.

Finally, an argument could be made that if "only X percent" of job-hunters find their jobs through the Net, the lesson isn't that you shouldn't use the Internet when job-hunting; it just means that you shouldn't spend more than X percent of your job-hunting time online, and should spend the rest of your time using other methods. As you go about the various aspects of your job-hunt, you will quickly get a sense of what is working, and what is a waste of your time. And this will apply to the Internet, too.

But let's say it one last time: your use of the Internet is *one* approach to the job-hunt, *one* part of an overall strategy. This book will help you to implement that strategy, but the strategy itself is to be found in the pages of *What Color Is Your Parachute?* So if you have not read *Parachute,* then you should put this book down right now and run out and buy a copy immediately (or . . . order one online). Read it cover to cover. Then you will find *this* book far more useful, and your overall job-hunt much more effective.

PARTS OF THE INTERNET

In order to speak effectively about job-hunting on the Internet, we should define exactly what we mean when we speak of the Internet. The Net has different parts, divided by function; three of them are useful in your job-hunt.

The Web

Many people—perhaps most—say "Internet" when what they really mean is the World Wide Web (WWW). This is the part that is primarily responsible for the tremendous growth of the Internet in recent years. The Web consists of the hyperlinked pages that you view with a browser, such as Internet Explorer or Netscape. By clicking on a link in the page you are currently viewing, you can be instantly transported to another page, which may be on a computer next door or on the other side of the planet. The process is transparent, the serving computer's actual location trivial. The Web is where you will find most of the data available to you. When speaking of "websites," "sites," "pages," and so on, we are referring to the World Wide Web.

A good way to think of the Web is as an almost infinite series of library rooms, each with many doors; as you enter through one door, you may find yourself in a room with many books in it, some useful, others not. You can read the data in this particular room, or you may choose to pass through one of the available doorways, to find yourself in other rooms, each with more books and more doorways. Maybe the information in the new room is more useful to you than in the last; perhaps not. You may stay and read, or, if you want, go back to one of the rooms you were already in, where there were other doors, to other library rooms, each with interesting possibilities for you to try. Some of the rooms are small; some are huge. Some rooms are filled with fascinating books; others may be useless. Some contain information that can be wrong, even offensive. Some rooms exist solely to serve as gateways to other rooms. Ultimately, all of the rooms, all over the World Wide Web, are interconnected with each other; hence, the name.

No one agrees on how many "rooms" there are for job-hunting on the Web; the figure most often mentioned is forty thousand, but this is really just the roughest of guesses. Yet, even if no one agrees on the *number* of job-hunting sites, everyone agrees on the *purpose* of these sites: to make it easier for job-hunter and employer to find each other. To this end, there are websites that are dedicated specifically to helping job-hunters and employers hook up directly. There are others that are dedicated to teaching people the techniques of job-hunting (using the Net and otherwise). There are sites dedicated to helping people find other people with common interests, geographies, education, fields of employment, and so on (the list is practically endless). There are sites useful for researching companies, fields, people, and places, as well as

anything else pertaining to what you want to do, where you want to do it, and how you might go about it. And if you are feeling a bit fuzzy on any of these matters, there are sites that offer counseling, testing, and advice for the job-hunter. As well, it seems that, lately, all but the smallest of companies have their own websites; most of these sites have a section dedicated to the company's labor needs, which may fit with your employment needs.

Email

In addition to the Web, the Internet has email capabilities. Most people use programs like Outlook or Eudora, or services such as AOL or MSN, to send and receive email. Depending on your Internet Service Provider (ISP, for short—modern technology has made acronyms as common as slang), you may also be able to use your Web browser for email.

If you are fairly new to the Internet, you will quickly find yourself dependent on email's quickness, convenience, and wide reach. Whether the powers-that-be ever fix the spam problem or not, email will continue to be the part of the Internet that has the greatest daily impact on the greatest number of people.

Usenet

One more part of the Net may be useful to you in your job-hunt; this is the Usenet newsgroup. You access newsgroups by using a newsreader (surprise!) such as Free Agent or Xnews; computer veterans refer to these programs as "clients." Though not as complete in available features, most Web browsers also have newsreader capabilities built in, and Google now indexes many newsgroups, allowing you to access them the same way you would look at any website.

Newsgroups are like little chat rooms, where people with similar interests can post articles, comments, gripes, pictures, and, occasionally, even news. The number of newsgroups that you will have access to depends on your ISP, but rarely will it be less than

10,000; mine allows me to view over 36,000. I said, *thirty-six thousand*. Different groups, based on different subjects.

Some of the subjects are quite general, such as people who are interested in photography. Others are more narrow in scope, such as people who are interested in black-and-white photography of mountains in Southern Chile or who listen to Christian holocaust metal music. This helps to explain the thirty-six thousand figure.

An unfortunately large number of newsgroups are devoted to the less noble aspects of human nature, but some are devoted to job-hunting. Regardless of your occupation or field of interest, there is undoubtedly a newsgroup devoted to it, where you can find others with the same interests as you. There you may make the contacts or find the information that will help you land your next job.

There are two drawbacks to this part of the Internet. The first is that there are so many newsgroups that finding the ones that will help you in your job-hunt can be difficult. The other drawback is that, to be honest, there is a lot of dreck posted in newsgroups. If nothing else, the Net has given everyone with a computer and a phone line complete equality to say whatever they want (and as much) to the whole wired world.

COMMON SENSE AND THE INTERNET

The wide reach of the Internet has brought great benefits, but the Net is not without its risks as well. These mainly fall into three categories: criminality, nuisance advertising, and bad information. All demand that you use care when on the Net.

The ability to bring all of this wonderful information to your desktop may also serve to bring the criminal element into your home or office. To guard yourself against those who would take advantage of you, you must follow a few simple guidelines.

Make sure that you understand the security settings on your computer, and use them appropriately. Do not download programs from sources you are unfamiliar with; make sure that you have current anti-virus software, and use it correctly. Use passwords whenever possible; make them obscure enough that they are unlikely to be guessed but not so obscure that you are likely to forget them. It helps to write your passwords down, but *don't store them on your computer.*

The behavior of Internet advertisers can be astonishing. On the milder side, you will find that these days, many websites—even good ones—have pop-up ads, and they can be a tremendous nuisance. Do not click anywhere in the pop-up except on the "close" box of the ad. Consider getting a pop-up blocker program—but buy one at the computer store. Many of the ones available for download on the Net are wolves in sheep's clothing.

That brings us to bad information.

A Cautionary Tale for the Internet Age

Recently, the city councilors in Alisa Viejo, California, scheduled a vote on whether to ban Styrofoam cups at city events, because they learned that Styrofoam manufacture involves the use of dihydrogen monoxide, or DHMO. Evidently, they found much of their information at a website dedicated to educating the public about the dangers of this chemical, located at `www.dhmo .org/facts.html`. And the information is frightening indeed. Consider:

- As stated on the website, "DHMO is a constituent of many known toxic substances, diseases and disease-causing agents, environmental hazards and can even be lethal to humans in quantities as small as a thimbleful."

- Inhaling even a small amount of DHMO can cause death.

- The gaseous form of DHMO can cause severe burns on human skin.

- Prolonged exposure to solid DHMO causes severe tissue damage.

- DHMO is a major component of acid rain.

- Research conducted by award-winning U.S. scientist Nathan Zohner concluded that roughly 86 percent of the population supports a ban on dihydrogen monoxide.

No wonder the Alisa Viejo city council wanted to remove all associations with this dangerous chemical.

The problem is that dihydrogen monoxide is another way of saying H_2O, or water. And it is all true: water is a major component of acid rain; breathing even small amounts will kill you, though we usually call it drowning; the gaseous form, known as "steam," can cause burns; prolonged direct exposure to the solid form (ice) causes tissue damage, known as "frostbite." As for Nathan Zohner, he *is* an award-winning scientist. He won a science fair when he was fourteen years old (he might be seventeen by now). When he told people about the dangers of DHMO, and asked fifty people if they thought it should be banned, forty-three of them said yes.

Although that's a fun example to bring up, I have a point here. We are used to trusting what we read. The economic realities of book, newspaper, and magazine publishing (with some help from the libel laws) have helped to ensure that most published information is generally trustworthy. When the trust is broken—as with reporters Jayson Blair of the *New York Times* and Jack Kelley of *USA Today*—it is major news itself.

But now we have the Internet. And even more than the printing press, the Net is the Great Equalizer; you can create and maintain a website for less money than most children's allowances these days. That means that the truth bar may be high, or it could be dropped on the floor with a loud *clang*. And there usually is no one, other than yourself, who can tell you where the bar is at any given moment.

Obviously, the DHMO website is a satire; it is not meant to intentionally mislead. And the vast majority of things you will read on the Net are at least *believed* to be true by the people who write and publish them . . . but that doesn't mean the information is always accurate. So when you are on the Net, use some care: try to confirm your data with multiple sources; consider the provenance of the information, who wrote it and why. When using Internet-based information for your job-hunt, take extra care to make sure it is correct.

STARTING YOUR JOB SEARCH

If you are new to the Internet, and you feel you need to know more before beginning your job search, consider reading chapter 6 of this book first, to give you some foundation for your Internet explorations. Also, try going to the following sites:

Basic Web Lessons
`www.aarp.org/learninternet`

From the good folks at AARP, the best tutorial for beginners I have found.

Beginner's Central
`www.northernwebs.com/bc/index.html`

If there is *anything* you want to know about the Internet and how to use it—email, browsers, file downloading, the Web, FTP, and more—it's all here, complete and very well written. The writer assumes you know almost nothing about the Internet, and builds from there.

When beginning your Internet job-hunt, it is helpful to start at the Gateways, for that is where you will find the largest amount of useful information in the least amount of time. And just what is a Gateway?

Gateways are simply explained: if you were to start from scratch, and go looking for job-hunting sites on the Internet, you would probably go to your favorite search engine, type in such keywords as: "careers," "jobs," "employment," "resumes," and so forth, and see what turned up. What you would get would be an avalanche—a huge mass of sites, some good, many not, in no particular order, badly needing sifting, organizing, evaluating, and such, before the list would be of any use to you.

But lucky you! A number of people have already done the job for you of searching, sifting, organizing, and evaluating. Their data is posted on websites I call "Gateways."

The best Gateways are well-organized information clearing-houses. They have articles about various aspects of the job-hunt, where you can learn more about the *process* of job-hunting, and how to go about it effectively. They have links to other sites on the Web where you can get more specific information, relevant to your particular job-hunt. The links you will find at these Gateways have all been vetted by knowledgeable people, so you will save huge amounts of time and energy by going to them first, rather than trying to sift through the avalanche of information that a search engine would provide.

Here are a few of the best:

Job-Hunt
www.job-hunt.org

One of the best Gateways, run by Susan Joyce. Here you will find a wealth of information on job-hunting, using the Internet effectively, and current articles about the world of work. In addition, there are many links to job-search resources and industry journals, organized by field, location, and so on. Job-Hunt also has a newsletter, the *Online Job Search Guide,* which is published by email twice a month. You can sign up for free; past issues are also available online at the site. This site is extremely well organized;

I find that the *look* of a website is crucial to using that site well, and finding the information that it has to offer. I really like the look of Job-Hunt.

JobStar
www.jobstar.org

Originally a California site—and still somewhat CA-centric—JobStar has a national presence, with lots of good information for the job-hunter. Run by Mary-Ellen Mort (who goes by the pseudonym "Electra" on the site), JobStar is particularly good when looking for information on salaries and the Hidden Job Market. (If you don't know what I mean by that, you have obviously *not* read *What Color Is Your Parachute?* and shame on you.) Since the site's funding is from the California State Library, there are links to actual job postings in California, with specific JobStar sites for Los Angeles, San Diego, Sacramento, and San Francisco; this also explains why there are not specific sites for areas outside of California. But JobStar does have links to help you find work, regardless of location, and most of the site's information is relevant, no matter where you live. Definitely one of the best job-hunting sites on the Web.

The Riley Guide
www.rileyguide.com

An extremely comprehensive site, thanks to its creator, Margaret F. Dikel (formerly Margaret Riley). What you get here is a well-organized, manageable index of job-hunting resources on the Internet, plus a lot of extras, like a summary of resume databases and job-search guides. In addition to informative (and timely) articles, there are many links to job listings by industry and profession, from "Academic Librarians" to "Zoo and Aquarium."

If I were to note any weakness in the site, it would be its completeness (which, of course, is also one of its main strengths). There is a *lot* of information here, and it may take you a little while to become familiar enough with the site to find exactly what you want. But this is a minor complaint; all things being equal, the Riley Guide is one of the best places to start your job-hunt.

CollegeGrad.com
www.collegegrad.com

This is self-billed as "the #1 entry-level job site." Believe it. Every time I go on this site, I find something else to pleasantly surprise me. Among its features is a large database of employers who are looking for grads and entry-level personnel; also, author Brian Krueger's book, *College Grad Job Hunter,* is on the site—complete, well translated to Web (hyperlinked) format, and free.

Part of the secret to the site's excellence is that the people here see their mission as a limited one: helping to find employment for college students and recent graduates *only*. But many of the site's resources are useful to all, and you should have the site in your Favorites (Bookmarks) folder for sure.

Quintessential Careers
www.quintcareers.com
www.quintcareers.com/portal.html

There is a *lot* of stuff here—more than two thousand pages, much of it quite good. Besides all of the stuff you would expect on a Gateway site, like articles on job-hunting, resumes, testing, and career assessment, you'll find data on making a career change, the top companies to work for (grouped in categories, like private companies, public companies, multicultural companies, companies that are best for the older worker, and so on), links to resources for teens, for the working college student . . . see? *Lots* of stuff. Also, the site has many links to colleges and other education resources. The interface is good, the pages well set up, and the site is logical and, for the most part, easy to use.

Not that the site is perfect. Many of the articles lack depth, though you can usually find links to more data when that's required. Also, if you use Netscape as your browser, some parts of this site will not work properly; you must use Microsoft Internet Explorer. The folks at Quintessential Careers have set up the site as a small version of Monster or HotJobs, with the ability to post a resume in the database or search for jobs. I found this part of the site to be slow when it worked, and it sometimes didn't work at all. For this reason and others, I recommend that you use the site as a resource for finding information, but if you want a job-hunting database, there are better ones available.

CareerOneStop
`www.careeronestop.org`

Sponsored by the U.S. Department of Labor, CareerOneStop is part of an interlinked network called America's Labor Market Information System, or ALMIS (this *is* the government, after all). CareerOneStop is the network's Gateway. Here you will find America's Job Bank (see Supersites below), where you can search a free database of jobs and resumes; Career InfoNet, where you can find information about employment trends, training, financial aid, state resources, and links to 6,500 websites with career information; and America's Service Locator, where you can find various job-hunting resources—information on companies, schools, and state employment development departments—near you.

Job-Hunter's Bible
`www.jobhuntersbible.com`

Don't forget the official site for readers of *What Color Is Your Parachute?* Here you will find many articles, links, advice, and resources for the job-hunter. Additionally, you will find a list of every Internet site and URL listed in this book. If you make Job-

Hunter's Bible your home page during your job search, you will be able to reach every resource listed in this book with a single mouse click.

Jobs and Careers Web Directory
`www.careers.org/index.html`

When it's 3 A.M. and you can't sleep, you've tried all the obvious job-related stuff on the Net, and you're thinking "Is that all there is?" (though I can't imagine that you would)—this is the place to go. The site claims six thousand links (on over five hundred pages) to jobs, employers, newspapers, Internet newsgroups, colleges, libraries, state employment offices, business, education, and career service professionals on the Web . . . the list goes on and on. Additionally, it has links to what I call "Day in the Life" stuff for the job-hunter, such as where to go to get a free checking account, what credit cards are cheapest, and so on.

SUPERSITES

Undoubtedly, there are some of you who are desperate to start your job-hunt *now,* and you don't have the time to read the rest of the book. Or maybe you believe you know everything about job-hunting already, and you just need to know where to start. If this describes you, then I hereby give you the Supersites.

The Supersites are the ones that just about everyone thinks of when you mention Internet job-hunting: Monster, CareerBuilder, HotJobs, America's Job Bank. These sites are hugely popular. In June of 2004—one month alone—9.6 million job-seekers were online with Monster; CareerBuilder was right behind, with 9.3 million. A recent survey showed that of all people who were job-hunting online, 89 percent had registered with Monster. Similar figures exist for the other Supersites.

At their core, like most job sites, the Supersites are *matching engines.* These are basically search engines that use keywords in your resume as the search term, and try to match these to a database of existing job postings. The Supersites wrap these matching engines in a package with articles and other services to assist the job-hunter.

We know that these sites are popular; but what we don't know is this: of the people who use these sites, how many get jobs? There is no recent, reliable data to tell us how effective the Supersites are. And since they are just matching engines—though extremely *popular* matching engines—the real question is, how effective are matching engines, in general, at getting people jobs?

There is no definitive answer. In order for matching engines to work well, they need to have a lot of data to match. Said another way, if you are trying to match your resume to a job posting, your chances of success increase as the number of postings increases. The same goes for employers: they are far more likely to fill a job opening if they have lots of people to choose from.

That said, it makes sense that the more popular a site is, the more likely that both job-hunters and employers will find what they are looking for there. If you think about it, the ideal situation would be if there were only one place where people went to post resumes and job listings—*all* job-hunters would be there, as would all job openings. If the job you were looking for existed, that is where you would find it. If the right person for an opening was on the planet (and looking for a job), bingo, same result.

Well, we're never going to have just one place where we match employers and job-hunters, but the arithmetic says that the next best thing would be to go to the most popular matching engines, with the largest databases, and that means the Supersites.

Readers of *Parachute* will know that employers—like job-hunters—like to take the shortest route between two points, as well as the least expensive. When they have a position that needs filling, they first try to hire from within; then they ask their current employees if they know of anyone suitable; then they go to their contacts (their "network"); and it is only when these other methods all fail that they will decide to spend money on filling a vacancy. Posting a job opening with one of the Supersites costs the employer money. So, statistically speaking, the job postings that are on the Supersites tend to be openings that are just a little harder to fill than otherwise, from the employer's point of view, because they would happily fill them without spending the money, if they could. From the job-hunter's point of view, this means that the jobs that many Supersite postings represent can be slightly less desirable, or require higher levels of experience and education.

Historically, the Supersites have worked better for those in the information technology field than those without (though as time passes, they are starting to show some effectiveness for those with executive, managerial, and technical backgrounds). They have been not very effective at all for low-tech and manufacturing jobs, and what we traditionally have called "blue-collar" workers. Recently, as more people have come to the Net to conduct their job-hunt, the Supersites' effectiveness has increased, although there is still no real data to say how much. Nor is it possible to say what the future holds. Still, I believe that the Supersites are worth trying (particularly if the job you are looking for is one likely to be found there). I don't think you should *only* use the Supersites, nor should you spend most of your Internet time there. The "extras" that they have for helping job-hunters are, for the most part, done better at sites like Job-Hunt, JobStar, and the Riley Guide. Also, many of the extras on the Supersites will cost you money, where the same services and quality (if not better) may be found elsewhere for free. But occasionally, you will find gems on the Supersites, and it is also possible that they will work perfectly for you. Just go there—like everywhere else on the Internet—with your eyes wide open.

Monster
www.monster.com

Arguably the best known of all the job-hunting sites on the Internet, Monster has many thousands of job listings, from all over the United States. Besides allowing you to search these listings by keyword, geographic area, and industry, Monster also has a Job Search Agent, which is a software program that will examine new listings as they are created, and will email you potential jobs that match your criteria. In a few test searches, without regard to location, I found more than 5,000 listings for registered nurses, 2,600 positions for electronic technicians, more than 1,200 listings for truck drivers (though most were just ads from truck-driving schools), and 4 positions for cabinetmakers. There were 70 nationwide positions for research biologists and more than 5,000 positions for CPAs.

Monster has other resources as well. These include:

- A free weekly newsletter, *Monster Careers,* as well as other (also free) newsletters concerning specific industries, careers, special interests, and "diversity and inclusion" groups (Native American, women, gays, and so on).

- Various "centers," with articles and discussions on resumes, career choices, public service, and so on; in some cases, these lead to services that Monster or its advertisers offer on a fee basis.

- Monster Networking—a system whereby you can meet other Monster job-hunters online, with whom you may develop mutually beneficial ties.

- Career and personality tests online; some are free, others are offered by sponsors on a fee basis.

As mentioned above, most of the job-hunting resources that Monster offers are done better at the Gateway sites . . . but not everything. There is a lot here that is helpful.

Monster's basic services are free to the job-hunter, although you must register; it is funded by employers' job listings and by online advertisers (with some pop-up ads). Much of what is good about Monster has to do with its size alone, but it also a well-thought-out and -designed job site.

Yahoo! HotJobs
`htto://hotjobs.yahoo.com`
`http://hotjobs.yahoo.com/careertools`

This is not the largest of the Supersites by far, but it offers a better-than-average selection of articles and links to resources for job-hunters, including information on salaries, resume writing, interviewing, and relocating. Although there are some for-fee services scattered among the links, most of the stuff here is free. You can sign up to receive their *Work Sheet* newsletter, as well as specialized newsletters for various fields of interest, such as health care, sales, finance, and so on. All newsletters are by email, and are free.

You will quickly notice that there is something missing in HotJobs' database of job listings: ads. While all of the other Supersites accept "job listings" from agencies and recruiters—which are often not real jobs at all—HotJobs only accepts listings from principals. As with the other Supersites, employers are charged to list their job openings or to search resumes, while services are free to the job-hunter once you register. (HotJobs doesn't seem to have any mechanism for culling out old accounts and user names, so you might have to go through the registration page a few times before you find a user name that has never been used at one time or another.) In my brief sampling of jobs in this database, I found more than a thousand postings each for nurses and CPAs (when returning results, the HotJobs search engine is not specific about numbers over one thousand), thirty-two electronics techs, no research biologists, and ninety cabinetmakers. (When comparing these figures to the other Supersites, remember that HotJobs' listings are all real jobs, not ads.)

HotJobs brings Yahoo!'s resources and experience to the table in the community and networking arena. For example, you will see a list of about thirty-five professions—legal, telecommunications, government, health care, accounting and finance, the list goes on—where you can join in discussions with people seeking work in these various fields. As with all such chat facilities, you do need to choose what you read carefully; there is a lot of complaining here, but that aside, there is still information to be had and contacts to be made.

America's Job Bank
`www.ajb.dni.us`

If you want proof that the government occasionally does something right, you might start here. America's Job Bank is one of four interlinked sites, as noted under CareerOneStop (listed above in the Gateway sites section). The U.S. Department of Labor and the employment development departments of the fifty states sponsor this network; it is free to both employers and job-hunters. Last time I visited, there were more than 1.25 million jobs in the database and almost seven hundred thousand resumes.

Since a large number of the listings come from state employment development departments, this is not a bad place to go if you are looking for a job in state or local government, a school district, state-run secondary education, public utilities, and so forth. Not all of the jobs listed here are terrific, but there *are* a lot of them. In my little survey, I found almost 7,000 listings for CPAs, 415 for cabinetmakers, more than 30,000 for registered nurses, 1,700 for electronics technicians, and 250 for research biologists. However, I should mention that the matching engine software used by this site cuts an extremely wide swath: for example, the search for research biologist kicked back listings for archeologist and senior city planner, among others. You are allowed to sort the job listings by relevance to your search keywords, but there is still a lot of chaff to be culled out. As with the other Supersites, you can look for jobs based on various criteria, and there is an automatic Search Scout that will email you as possible job listings come in that match your criteria.

The associated research site, America's Career InfoNet (which can be reached through the Job Bank site, or separately at `www.acinet.org`), allows you to research employment trends, careers, training, education, financial aid and scholarships, relocation issues, wages and salaries, and so on. There is a library of career articles, links to testing and assessment, and a Career Resource Library with sixty-five hundred links to other sites with career information on the Net. This site is well laid out and well thought out, and I think it is worth saying again: it is free to both employers and job-hunters. Moreover, the site is slow to point you to other resources that are fee based; sadly, the same cannot be said for all of the Supersites.

Possibly more than with the other job boards, you should be careful about the currency of job listings on America's Job Bank. Not all employers pull their listings once they are filled. Before applying for a position that is some weeks old, confirm that it is still a viable opening.

CareerBuilder
www.careerbuilder.com

CareerBuilder is owned jointly by the Tribune Company, Gannett, and Knight-Ridder—newspaper companies all. This means that it not only accepts paid postings from employers, but the database also has want ads from around two hundred newspapers across the country. As a result, the database is huge, and because of the newspaper origin of many of the postings, you will find more lower-tech and traditionally blue-collar jobs listed here. In my unscientific sampling, I found positions for 25 cabinetmakers, 3,300 truck drivers (again, most were ads), close to 22,000 registered nurses, 980 electronic techs, more than 5,000 CPAs, and 87 research biologists.

Registering with the site allows you to search its database by keyword, field, and location; the site offers newsletters and other services. Because of its newspaper background, this site also partners with websites that offer apartment rentals, autos for sale, and networking (through Tribe.net) across the country. You can sign up to receive emailed information about career fairs in your area, as well as for the *Cool Jobs* newsletter, which highlights certain jobs and companies that use CareerBuilder for hiring.

This site is more commercially oriented than the other Supersites, and there are certainly more pop-up ads. I was struck by the Resources page; the vast majority of links on the page lead to a fee-based offer rather than to the more typical free Internet resource.

Research on the Internet

It is a rare job-hunt that does not require some research. And, as the salary level rises, as the required experience and skill set of the applicant goes up, as the responsibility inherent in the prospective job increases, so does the amount of research required to identify the field, the job, and the company you would most like to work for, along with the person there who has the power to hire you. As I mentioned in chapter 1, a 2003 study showed that of those companies that hired through the Net, 59 percent of their hires were through the company's own website—four times as many people as were hired through Internet job boards. In a world where the Internet is accounting for more and more job-hunting activity, this means that you *must* be able to identify your skills, research the fields and industries where your skills can be used, locate the companies in those industries near you, and identify those companies you are interested in working for.

Luckily, research is one of those tasks for which the Internet was born. Often, it is a researcher's dream: a worldwide library at your fingertips, which you can access anytime, day or night, in your frumpiest clothes, without ever leaving your home.

But you must do your research with care and intelligence. There is *so* much information available on the Internet that you can be easily overwhelmed; and you must know how to use the Net properly in order to separate the good stuff from the bad. Too

much information is just as bad as no information. But this trail has been blazed: a number of tools have been developed to help you find what you need in this vast sea of data.

DIRECTORIES

There are places where you will find hundreds to thousands of websites organized by subject; these are called "directories." Unlike search engines (see below), where results are determined by software, directories are organized by hand. To truly appreciate the difference between directories and search engines, think of the difference between browsing and searching. Directories are hierarchically organized by subject; you start with a general heading and move toward more specific groupings. Conversely, a search engine looks for data that will fit with certain keywords, regardless of subject. Directories are for when you kind of vaguely know what you are looking for but need some ideas to help you narrow things down; or when you are looking at general subjects, such as careers, sports, movies, space flight—like that. (Though there are specialized directories as well.)

As I said, data is organized by subject, and there are many subjects. When you are looking for data on the Internet, a directory is often the best place to start. Even if you don't find exactly what you are looking for, the subject categories themselves can help you with ideas on what keywords to use if you must move on to the search engines.

Bear in mind when using directories, as with search engines, one size does not fit all. Just because you didn't find it in one does not mean that it isn't in another. Also, since they are compiled by human hand, the entries are not always as current as we might like . . . but you'll find a lot of variety between different directories.

Open Directory Project

`www.dmoz.org`
`www.dmoz.org/Business/Employment/Careers`

The largest directory on the Web, with over 4.4 million sites in close to 600,000 subject categories. As the name implies, this is an all-volunteer project (as I write, there are 64,000 people involved in compilation and editing). On the one hand, this allows the directory to gain its large size, but it also means that some entries may not be as up-to-date as you might hope. Also, since each entry is examined and reviewed by a real person, and there are *lots* of these real persons involved, there may be some slight bias now and then on the part of the editors, who, for the most part, are not professionals. Still, this is the obvious place to start when you are looking for subject information. As an example of the site's depth, check out the Careers page (URL above).

Yahoo!

`http://dir.yahoo.com`
`http://dir.yahoo.com/Business_and_Economy/`
`Shopping_and_Services/Employment/`
`Career_Counseling`

One of the best-known sites on the Internet, for many reasons, Yahoo! still has the best directory for a commercial site. Some entries are "sponsored," obviously, but they are clearly marked (and occasionally useful themselves). As you know, Yahoo! also has a search engine (see below), and you can limit your search to the Yahoo! directory.

As an example of the difference between commercial and non-commercial sites, compare the Careers page at Open Directory Project with the Career Counseling page at Yahoo!

Resource Discovery Network
`www.rdn.ac.uk`
`www.sosig.ac.uk/roads/subject-listing/`
`World-cat/busent.html`

Not a single directory, but a network (duh) of more specialized directories, all excellent. For example, the site links to the Social Science Information Gateway for business subjects (the URL for business/company research is above); there, you can click on the entry title for a précis of the site, or you can click on an icon next to the entry to be taken directly to the site.

The RDN is an example of what is called a "closed directory." On open directory sites, such as the Open Directory Project or Yahoo!, you can suggest sites to be included; at some directories, websites can pay to be listed. At closed directories, the entries are vetted by professionals, usually librarians, so the quality of the data you find will tend to be better ... sometimes *much* better.

Librarian's Index to the Internet
`http://lii.org`

Another closed directory, and probably the best on the Net. Entries have the date that they were last looked at by one of the directory's staff, so you will know how recent their site descriptions are. Next to Yahoo!, probably the most-used directory on the Net.

CHAPTER TWO

Internet Public Library
`www.ipl.org`

Another excellent directory. Not always a lot of depth here, but the entries tend to be current and authoritative and worth checking out for your research.

Though not related directly to job-hunting, one of the areas of the IPL that I like best is the Reading Room, with links to books published on the Net. Want to read the *Iliad*? Maybe an actual first edition of *Huckleberry Finn* with the original E. W. Kemble illustrations? How is this going to help your job-hunt? I don't know; forget I mentioned it.

InfoMine
`http://infomine.ucr.edu`

The directories listed above are all general directories (well . . . the Resource Discovery Network is actually a network of slightly more specialized directories, but you get the idea). There are many specialized directories on the Internet, as well. How do we find these directories? Why, we look in a directory *directory*, of course.

InfoMine is halfway between a directory and a search engine. When you tender a query, rather than kick back pertinent Web pages, it will return resources—databases, libraries, directory sites, and so forth—where you are likely to find the kind of information you are looking for. You can specify the types of resources you want to search; in many cases, you can also browse through the resource types.

SEARCH ENGINES

The Internet is huge, to the point of virtual endlessness; it is like a library where there is no card index, and no titles on the book spines. No one can ever know everything that is there, at any given moment. Imperfect though it may be, the best tool we currently have for finding *specific* information on the Internet is the search engine.

There are many search engines on the Net. Some are better than others; in certain cases, *much* better. To understand why, and pick the best engine(s) for your research, we need to look at how search engines do what they do.

It's a gross oversimplification, but a search engine is a bit like the Find command in your word processor. When you want to find a certain part of a document, you enter a keyword into the Find command, and the word processor software looks for a match.

That's kind of the way search engines work. In their case, you could say that the Internet is the document . . . but it's actually more complex than that, and it is in this complexity that we find the differences between the many search engines available. The differences can be broken down into three factors:

- The way they index the Web.

- The way they search the index, return results, and rank them (by how closely the engine thinks they match your query—the "relevance").

- The way they deal with advertising and "sponsored matches."

These three factors affect the quality of the results that the search engine will return to you when you make a search query. Let's look at each more closely:

The Way They Index the Web: Search engines are computer programs that prowl the Internet (using a software tool called a "crawler" or "spider"), and create a database of pointers to various Web pages (millions of them). Then, when a researcher—say, you, for instance—comes along and says, "Find me data on subject X," the search engine kicks out addresses from its indexed database, from which it has located information it thinks is relevant to your request.

The algorithms (a programmer's way of saying "methods") that the different search engines use to index the Web can vary significantly from one search engine to another. This means that each search engine's data index will be very different, and that affects how each responds to your search queries.

The Way They Search the Index: Search engines do not search the Internet directly; they search the database they have compiled about the Internet, using their spiders. So, even if two search engines are using the same search technology (very common), the databases that they are using to find your search results are not the same. (In other cases, different engines use different technology to search the same databases, again yielding different results.) Nor are these technologies, and the algorithms they use, equal in effectiveness, and this means that some search engines are more effective at finding *your* data than others. There is overlap, of course, but the overlap is far from complete. This means that when you are conducting an information search, you should not depend on a single engine to give you all of the information that is available out there.

The Way They Deal with Advertising and Sponsored Matches: All of the search engines are there to make money. Some will return, along with your search results (but clearly separate), a list of short ads from companies that offer products and services that are usually somewhat related to your search results; it's a kind of targeted advertising. (Google and Yahoo! use this approach.) Other search engines return results to your queries that are actually from websites that have paid to be returned as search results (often called "sponsored matches"), but these results are clearly marked as sponsored; AltaVista and Overture are examples. Still others mix in sites that have paid to be included into your search results, *without telling you which ones are sponsored,* regardless of whether those sites rank high in relevance to your search query. According to the U.C. Berkeley Library, MetaCrawler does this, as do others. I don't personally find this ethical, but there it is, and you should be aware of it. Nothing will skew your search for data as badly as having sponsored results mixed in with what I term "relevant results," if you don't know which is which.

Using Search Engines

As noted above, one of the key differences among the various search engines is how they rank the data they have culled from the Web and prioritize it for your search query—you *did* want the most relevant results first, rather than buried here and there in a thousand pages of URLs, right? This is the secret sauce of the search engine field, and it is what determines how good your search results are, and how happy *you* are with a particular search engine.

But part of the responsibility is yours. To a certain degree, you must understand the language that search engines speak if you want to use them most effectively. For example, if you want to learn about job-hunting, you could just go to a search engine, and type this:

job hunting

But done that way, most search engines just kick out articles that have both the word *job* and the word *hunting,* but not necessarily both words together. You may get results that include references to someone who makes his living by stalking moose up by the Arctic Circle. But if you enclose the two words in quotes, like this:

"job hunting"

then the search engine will know that it's a phrase, and the results will be closer to what you want. It still may include someone who has a *job* that involves *hunting.* Of course, you could have typed:

"job hunting" NOT animals

and that will eliminate most of the results that are not related to finding employment.

Here's another example. Suppose you want the search engine to only search in one website for your target phrase. You could then type in this:

"job hunting" site: `www.jobhuntersbible.com`

and the search engine would only return results from the Job-Hunter's Bible website.

Simple stuff, easy to learn and use. And of course, you can accomplish much the same thing by going to the advanced search page that every engine has. If you are doing a lot of research, however, you will save yourself lots of time if you learn the language that the search engines speak. To this end, I direct you to a few places where you can learn more about using search engines and their language:

Web Searching Tutorial
`www.askscott.com/tindex.html`

This is one of the best tutorials on Web search engines that I have found. Easy to understand, yet very complete.

University at Albany: A Primer in Boolean Logic

`http://library.albany.edu/internet/`
`Boolean.html`

When structuring search queries, it's helpful to understand how Boolean logic works, since this is how most search engines parse your requests. This explains how to structure your search queries for more effective results.

University of South Carolina: Basic Search Tips
`www.sc.edu/beaufort/library/pages/bones/`
`lesson7.shtml`

A quick intro on how to formulate search queries. There are links to finding more in-depth information, if you like.

Learn the Net
`www.learnthenet.com/english/html/77advanc.htm`

Offers a brief overview of concepts like phrase searching AND Boolean logic, but NOT very complete.

Search Engine Watch
`http://searchenginewatch.com`

This site is all about search engines. Very current; this site, more than any other, keeps its finger on the pulse of the search engine industry (and, yes, it is an industry; the aggregate profits are huge). You can find tips for using search engines, as well as information on specific engines—who uses whose database, who just bought up whom, what new features are being offered at a particular search site . . . like that.

Some search engines are better at finding certain types of data. We'll start with the general search engines; here are the ones I believe to be the best:

Google

`www.google.com`

Google has come to dominate the search engine arena on the Web, mainly because it does what it does better than the others do. In this case, "better" means that it is faster, that the results it offers are more likely to be relevant to your request, and that it will not mix in commercial results with legitimate data.

I like Google because it has a simple interface, yet it is no less effective for that. As a matter of fact, Google's interface and look has been copied by many, if not most, of the search engines on the Web.

But really, a lot of why I like Google is intangible and subjective. It just seems to return better, more relevant data than the other engines do. That's part of what I was saying earlier: because the different search engines use different algorithms to do what they do, and build different databases, some will be more effective than others. Google's rankings by relevance are usually best, to my taste. When I am doing a search, Google is the first place I turn.

When using Google, you may choose to target your search on the Web, through Google's collection of images, news, and so on. Many people don't know that Google has a directory feature that is similar to Yahoo!'s; you can find it at `www.google.com/dirhp`. In fact, there are many services at Google; visit the site's main index at `www.google.com/options/index.html` to see what I mean.

When a search engine indexes a page for its database, it will often keep a copy of the page on its server; this is called a "cached page." Google allows you to look at the cached version of the page, highlighting your search terms; it also tells you the date that the page was last looked at by the crawler and indexed. The best copy of the page, for your purposes, may not always be the most current version; the cached version may contain information that has since been removed or changed but is useful to you.

Google allows you to search in newsgroups, giving you access to data in one of the most difficult parts of the Internet. You can also search for businesses and services by geographic area, search specialized indexes of colleges, or the site's index of U.S government sites . . . you see what I mean? It will translate pages between French, English, German, Spanish, and Portuguese, and you can have Google display its interface in any one of 104 languages.

Google may not be the *only* search engine that offers many of these features (though some are clearly unique), but when you put it all together, Google deserves its reputation for being *the* search engine for the Web.

Teoma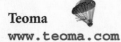
www.teoma.com

Owned by Ask Jeeves, which is a pretty good search engine as well (see below), Teoma—which means "expert" in Gaelic—currently has over 500 million pages in its database. That's a pretty good size, though it is far less than Google's and Yahoo!'s estimated four billion each. Teoma is also proud of its technology for ranking results in terms of relevance to your search query. Along with results returned, there is a Refine area, with suggestions for refining your search when the first results are not specific or relevant enough.

Another good feature in Teoma is that in the first page of results returned from a query, there will be a section labeled Resources—a good place for finding Web directories and searchable databases. Sponsored links are clearly marked as such.

Teoma's relevance ranking is similar to Google's, though not always the same. For example, Teoma ranks a page's relevance by how many other Web pages on the same subject are linked to it. Because it takes time for such links to form, ranging from hours to months, new items will not be ranked high for relevance on Teoma. For newer items, then, Google or Yahoo! Search work better.

Ask Jeeves
www.ask.com

This is Teoma's crawler, with a more natural, intuitive interface. Your queries can
be natural language questions, like,
"What's that piece of skin between your
thumb and first finger called?" (I never found
out, but pinching it is supposed to cure a headache.
Thanks, Jeeves.) If search engines frighten you and
Boolean logic escapes you, try here. What could be
threatening about an English butler?

Yahoo! Search
http://search.yahoo.com

It seems like Yahoo! has been around since the Internet itself. Until recently, it was using Google's search technology (though not its database), but it has recently unveiled
its own. When searching with Yahoo! Search, you
may choose for it to search the Web, Yahoo!'s own directory (Yahoo! has long been one of the largest portals
to the Web), the yellow pages, and/or other categories. When you
are doing a search, it is rare to not find something useful with a
combination of Google, Teoma, and Yahoo! as a one-two-three
punch (with Beaucoup, below, batting cleanup).

META-SEARCH TOOLS

Dogpile
www.dogpile.com

Dogpile is one of the meta-search engines, where your query is
submitted to a number of search engines, then a few of the returns from each are combined into a list of results. In practical
terms, you sacrifice depth for breadth . . . but that's not always a
bad thing. If you want to get a quick overview of what's available
for a certain search phrase, then a meta-search engine may be a
good idea.

Among the search engines that Dogpile uses are Google, Teoma, Yahoo!, and Ask Jeeves, as well as directories such as Look-Smart and the Open Directory. There are other engines and databases it uses to return a certain amount of commercial results.

Ah, commercial results . . . the Achilles' heel of the meta-search community. Some meta-search engines have a problem with mixing sponsored results in with editorial results. In this case, "editorial" means "real," and "problem" means it's a problem for the user, not the meta-site, and the reason it's a problem is that the sites don't always tell you which is which. This practice, which started out some years ago as a serious lapse in ethics, is now standard; and those who started it, once viewed as outcasts in the industry, are now considered "visionaries."

Luckily, there are some companies that don't put the almighty dollar first, and Dogpile is one of these: sponsored results are clearly marked as such. The site has some nice features: it remembers your last few searches; it suggests ways to refine your search; and you can choose where to focus your search—Web pages, multimedia, news, images, and so on. Because of the lack of depth, I believe that meta-searchers are of limited use—kind of between a directory and a normal search engine—but Dogpile is one of the best in the bunch.

Beaucoup
www.beaucoup.com

A little different from your basic meta-search engine, Beaucoup queries and returns results from Google, Yahoo!, AltaVista, Fast, Ask Jeeves, Lycos, MSN, WiseNut, HotBot, and AOL Search, and tells you from which each of its results came. You can also tell it to search only one of the engines at a time. However, since the meta-engines don't return all the results you would get directly from, say, Google, you should just go to the source rather than use Beaucoup this way. Sponsored results are clearly marked in a separate list from relevant results.

In addition to the search engines I listed, Beaucoup has other resources it can tap. There are some databases that you can direct the Beaucoup search engine toward.

You may not find a lot of depth here, but what you will find—heck, it's what meta-engines are *supposed* to do—is a tool that cuts broadly but not deeply. Once you start here, you can choose how to narrow your information hunt.

Profusion
`www.profusion.com`

Part meta-search engine, part directory, this site has a longer reach than many. Not only can you access the standard search engines, but the site gives you the ability to target the specific tools and databases you want to look at.

CLUSTERING

One of the most popular methods for ranking search engine results involves linking: how many other Web pages link to this one? The theory being, obviously, that if a lot of other pages link to a certain site, then they must like the data on this page. It's another way of saying that the data there has the ring of authority; of course, the converse may also be true: if no one links to it, maybe the online community doesn't think the data there is so great. It isn't foolproof, of course, and it isn't the only method for ranking results, but with many engines, it is the primary factor affecting what is at the top of the page (and what isn't) when a search engine returns the results of a query.

This has led to a practice known as "Google bombing." It doesn't take too many people with Web pages to get together and skew the ranking of the data that search engines return. In 2003, some people got together and caused the query phrase "miserable failure," when typed into the major search engines, to return President Bush's biography from the White House website. (And of course Bush supporters then Google bombed Hillary Clinton, Michael Moore, and others. You can read more about Google bombing at `http://en.wikipedia.org/wiki/Google _bomb` and `http://news.bbc.co.uk/2/hi/americas/ 3298443.stm`.)

Inevitably, companies will start using this technique to skew results so that they start getting more favorable ranking in search results, or cause their competitors to get lower rankings.

One approach that helps to reduce the effect of Google bombing is *clustering*. Some search engines, rather than returning results in strict hierarchical order, cluster the results under various headings. For example, a search on "tension" might bring results grouped under headings for politics, headaches, musical instrument strings, physics, and so on. When results are returned this way, it is harder to make any single site artificially jump out at you . . . and of course, it is often a better way to zero in on the data that you want.

Here are a few search engines that use clustering:

Clusty
`http://clusty.com`

An experimental beta site from Vivisimo, Clusty is a meta-search engine that allows you to choose the way your query results are clustered. Do you want it grouped by topic? By source? By URL? Like many search engines, sponsored results are at the top of the list, but they are clearly labeled and separated from relevant results.

Mooter
`www.mooter.com`

Mooter's clusters are presented as a graphical formation resembling the spokes of a wheel. You can choose one of the spokes, where the clusters are broken down even further . . . it's pretty interesting. I was a bit disappointed that Mooter seems to return more sponsored results than most of the clustering-type search engines.

Kartoo
`www.kartoo.com`

This site takes the graphical presentation of clusters one step further: if you have Macromedia's Flash player installed (easy enough to get if you don't, and installation is more or less automatic once you agree to the legal stuff), Kartoo also uses a graphical interface to show you not only the various clusters, but it also draws lines showing the various relationships between the

clusters. This can be fascinating all by itself; these relationships can give you new insight into how to find what you are looking for, and add meaning to the results returned.

Kartoo is not the fastest search engine on the Web, but it does have some neat features that I encourage you to explore. Not a bad addition to your toolkit as you are doing research for your job-hunt.

SEARCH ENGINE HELP

Before you use any of these search engines, you should know that each has its own little quirks and special features, so be sure to visit the help pages of the engine you are using. Here are the URLs for the ones I have listed:

Google

```
www.google.com/help/index.html
```

Teoma

```
http://sp.teoma.com/docs/teoma/about/
searchtips.html
```

Yahoo! Search

```
http://help.yahoo.com/help/us/ysearch
```

Ask Jeeves
```
http://static.wc.ask.com/docs/
announcements/searchsmarter.html
```
Dogpile
```
www.dogpile.com/info.dogpl/search/
help/index.htm
```
Beaucoup
```
www.beaucoup.com/beauhelp.html
```

SPECIALIZED SEARCH ENGINES

The search engines that I have recommended so far are all generalized search engines with large databases. However, there are a *lot* of smaller, specialized search engines out there. Remember, it is not the *technology* that characterizes the various search engines so much as their *databases*. It follows, then, that for a specialized search, you don't need specialized technology as much as you need a specialized database. Here are a few:

A Collection of Special Search Engines
```
www.leidenuniv.nl/ub/biv/specials.htm#Par62
```

A very extensive list of special search engines and searchable directories. I am continually amazed at the riches on this site.

All Search Engines
```
www.allsearchengines.com
```

The name is actually a bit misleading. In my time on this site, I have found it to be more of a directory than a search engine list, but of course there are hundreds of specialized search engines here as well. From a list of all U.S. government web servers, to where to do a reverse phone number lookup, to hundreds of career sites . . . there is a *HUGE* amount of stuff here. I particularly like the page of public libraries online, listed at `www.allsearchengines.com/libraries.html`, and the list of foreign search engines, grouped by country, at `www.allsearchengines.com/foreign.html`.

SearchEngines.com
www.searchengines.com

Not a search engine in itself, but a way to find the specialized search engines . . . kind of a search engine for search engines. Search engines on the site are organized in many ways, and you can find engines that are specific to certain countries or continents, ones that specialize in certain subject areas, and so on.

Search Adobe PDF
http://searchpdf.adobe.com

You are, of course, familiar with Adobe Acrobat and the Portable Document Format (PDF) files that it generates. Acrobat is the favorite format of many libraries for storing their data, due to its ability to store text and pictures on the same page, making a PDF file look just like any book, with, you know, pages? Made out of paper?

To a search engine, though, a PDF file page is an image—a picture, just like any picture of the beach or the mountains—and since the search engine spiders cannot scan a picture of the beach for your search term, the data contained in PDF files will not show up in your searches (although Google is a notable exception, as it is actively indexing PDFs, and can translate them into HTML for display).

Search Adobe PDF is a search engine just for PDF files. Since so much written material has been, and is being, translated into this industry-standard format, this site is an important resource, and one that should not be ignored in your research.

On the other hand, it is rare that you will find recent, time-sensitive material in Acrobat format. If your current search is for this type of data, you will probably want to mine other sources first. But much useful information—annual reports, financial data, and archived information, just to name a few types—will be found in PDF format, and might be available through searches on this site.

Earlier, I mentioned that search engines often cache the pages they index, and some give you the choice of viewing the cached version, or the actual page on the website where it was found. All of the PDF files I found at Search Adobe PDF were cached on its server, but the links to many of the original pages were broken. This is a clue that currency may be a problem with this site. But few others do what it does, and you should know that it's here when you need it.

BEYOND SEARCH ENGINES

Surprisingly, much of the Internet is beyond the reach of search engines; they will only give you access to between one-tenth and one-half of what is available. The rest is hidden unless you know where to look for it.

And in order to access this huge amount of data that search engines will not find for you, it is helpful to know *why* search engines are so limited in their reach. Much of it is too technical to list here, but in general terms, there are three basic reasons:

- The search engines are told by their masters not to go to certain areas. For example, there are large databases on the Net that it is not profitable to index, or the data is in a form that is difficult for the search engines to digest, or for other reasons, it just doesn't make economic sense.

- The search engines are told by the owners of the data to keep out. Not everyone wants to have their data indexed and available through Google or Yahoo! if it would, for instance, reduce their own profits to do so. There are commands that can be embedded in Web pages that tell the search bots to keep out.

- The search engines are not smart enough to find the data, or perhaps they cannot even find the website that stores the data. If nobody is linking to a certain website yet, the search bot may not even be able to find the site.

And yet, much of this data might be helpful to you in your jobhunt. Where is it, and how do you find it?

Databases

There is a huge amount of information available in databases on the Web. Once you find them, their information is usually easily accessible. Most have a human-oriented interface that allows you to find the data they contain.

But the real problem is, how do you find the databases? Try these techniques:

Try adding the words *database* or *archive* to your search engine inquiry. (An example might be "professional association AND database.") Even when the search engines haven't mined the information they contain, the engines usually know where the databases themselves are located.

Try URL mining. When you find a URL with a question mark in it, erase everything in the URL from the question mark to the end, then hit the Enter key. Occasionally you will turn up a database, or a link to one.

Other people on the Net often know where good databases are, and link to them . . . but rarely to just one. When you find a database, put the "link" command before its address, and plug that into a search engine. Although syntax varies from one engine to another, it will usually be something like

"link: `http://www.jobhuntersbible.com`"

This will return the Web addresses of all the sites that the search engine knows have links to that address. Go to those places and see where else those sites link to.

When Teoma returns search results, there will be a Resources group of addresses; though these are rarely databases themselves, they often point the way to them.

Use the subject directories listed earlier, like the Librarians Index to the Internet, the Open Directory Project, and so on. These will often point you to databases you can access.

Other Data Forms and FTP

Search engines often ignore page content that is not written in HTML, but that doesn't mean you should. For instance, try this with Google:

filetype: doc "career change older employee"

This would return the addresses of any documents written in Microsoft Word on that subject. Or instead of "doc," try "pdf" for Adobe Acrobat files, "xls" for Excel spreadsheets, and so on. In particular, Adobe Acrobat files can be a gold mine of information. Standard search engines won't always read them, and of those that do, size limits can make the contents invisible. For example, Yahoo! and Google both crawl PDF files, but will not index files greater than 500K and 100K, respectively. If the files are larger than that—not too difficult these days—the data inside doesn't exist, as far as these search engines are concerned. Yet you can still find the addresses of the documents themselves, using this technique, and open them yourself.

Before HTML, most data on the Internet was moved using a protocol called FTP, which stands for File Transfer Protocol. If you have ever gone to a site like the Virtual Software Library, TUCOWS, or the File Mine, in order to download a piece of shareware, it was transferred to your computer using FTP. Although the mechanism was hidden from you, the protocol is built into your browser, and you can get FTP files the same way you access HTML pages.

FTP can be valuable to your research because there is a *huge* number of files available on the Net that are not accessible through the Web per se. Many are at libraries, universities, and government archives. To find them, you have to prowl the sites they are on, clicking into directories to see what's there, and downloading any files that look like useful possibilities. Or you can go somewhere that knows where to find files that are FTP-accessible.

Tile.Net
http://tile.net/ftp

The best place to look for FTP sites is in the directory here at Tile.Net. Sites are listed by country of origin, as well as alphabetically. Clicking on a site name will take you to a summary page, which tells you where the computer is located, what kind of data you are likely to find there, any limits to the operating hours, email address of site administrator, and so on. If it looks like a good place, then click on the name listed after Site to access the FTP archives on that computer. (Note: there is a little bug in their software; if you look under the Country heading, sometimes you'll see just a series of bullets, with nothing to click on. Scroll down, and the names will appear.)

You won't be allowed in everywhere you try to go; not all of these are *anonymous* FTP sites ("anonymous FTP" indicates that the host computer doesn't care who you are). Other sites may allow you in, but restrict your access to certain directories. When this happens, you can often save time by going straight to the /pub directory, which is almost always open to the public. At other times, you will be asked for a password; if trying "password" or "public" doesn't get you in, leave it alone and go elsewhere. Don't trespass.

Now, bear in mind that FTP is an older way of transferring information on the Internet, and many—*many*—of the sites listed are no longer active. In some cases, you can do this:

• right-click on the archive name (all of you Macintosh users, of course, cannot right-click on anything; instead, hold down the Control key while you click)

• choose "copy link location" or "copy shortcut" from the pop-up menu

• paste this into your browser's address window

• edit the "ftp" part of the address to read "http"

• press the Enter key

You just changed the protocol by which you will communicate with the site, from the older file transfer protocol, to the newer hypertext transfer protocol, the language of the Web. Often, site administrators will have abandoned the FTP site and replaced it with a website, with the same information (and maybe, with newer stuff as well). Other times, the FTP site is still operable, but this is a good thing to try anyway, because there is often a Web version with the same (or newer) information available to you. This helps you find many websites you otherwise might not.

THE UNDERWEB

The part of the Internet that is beyond the reach of search engines is often called the UnderWeb, the Invisible Web, the Deep Web, and similar names. Here are some other places to look for data on the UnderWeb:

Dipsie
www.dipsie.com

As I write, this next-generation search engine is not yet available, but maybe that will change by the time you read this. Dipsie, according to reports, has a crawler that can penetrate much of the Web that other search engines cannot, thanks to new patent-pending technologies. Since it is not yet available, I cannot test it, so I cannot rate it for you, but when the site becomes operative, this may turn out to be a better search engine (or at least, one with a more far-reaching database) than anything previously available.

LibDex
www.libdex.com

This is an index to eighteen thousand libraries, many of which have online materials and databases that you can access.

Educator's Reference Desk Database
www.eduref.org/Eric

This is a database of over a million abstracts related to education, which covers a wide swath. You may use the database to locate the actual documents, find various libraries with more data available, or view the documents online if you choose to subscribe to that service.

Profusion
www.profusion.com

Listed above under meta-search engines, with this site, you have the ability to search many resources beyond the normal Web. Part meta-search engine, part directory, this site allows you to target the specific tools and databases you want to look at.

The Digital Library Project at U.C. Berkeley
`http://elib.cs.berkeley.edu`

A glimpse of the future, when *everything* is online. There is so much stuff here, that I am not going to bother describing it. Instead, when you have some time, start delving into what is available at the site.

Technical Communication Library
`http://tc.eserver.org`
`http://tc.eserver.org/sitemaps/`
`categories.lasso`

This is a site especially for technical writers. It's classic UnderWeb: there are many resources here, but it is unlikely that much of the library's content will show up in the results of most search engines . . . so you need to poke around a little. They have more than 8,500 articles and entries here, organized under various subjects and groupings. The second URL is a page where you can browse (or search) through the subjects; click on one, and the resources under that subject are listed. In this case, a "resource" could be an article, it could be a list of links, it could be a pointer to other databases like this one. Nice interface, too.

Resources and Databases—
Purdue University Library
`www.lib.purdue.edu/eresources`

Wow. An excellent page, directs you straight to many UnderWeb databases, grouped by subject. Also, take a look around the whole site while you are here; the library has a strong Web presence, with current information and many special features.

Academic Info Educational Subject Directory
`http://academicinfo.net`

A good directory with links to many databases.

Topica

`http://lists.topica.com`

The Internet has about a bazillion mailing lists for a bazillion newsletters, for people who are interested in roughly a bazillion different subjects. At Topica, nestled somewhere in the advertising, you will see a box that says, "Choose from Thousands of Newsletters and Discussions." Clicking on the subject headings will lead you to pages with even more subjects, which will eventually lead you to (just like it says) thousands of newsletters on thousands of subjects . . . all of which you can subscribe to, or otherwise access. I might have been exaggerating with the "bazillion" thing, but there *are* a lot of them.

Invisibleweb.net

`www.invisible-web.net`

Chris Sherman and Gary Price are the leading experts on researching below the visible surface of the Internet; their popular book *The Invisible Web* spawned this website, where you will find a good directory of UnderWeb resources. If you are going to be doing a lot of research on the Internet, both for your job-hunt and possibly for your eventual job, I highly recommend you get their book, which can be ordered from this site.

Amazon.com

`www.amazon.com`

Maybe you've heard of these guys? This is actually a good site to do certain types of research. The database, besides listing more than (fill in the blank, but make it big) books, often contains excerpts from same, and it's all searchable. Every now and then you can get a real gem here. I don't advocate this as the first place you should turn, but don't forget about it, either. (By the way, give the credit card to your spouse before doing any significant browsing here.)

ibiblio
`www.ibiblio.org`

An excellent digital archive. Most stuff is not directly related to job-hunting, of course, but who knows what you may, some day, need to know? Lots of data about language, literature, history, science.

Academic Info
`www.academicinfo.net`

Also not necessarily related, at least directly, to the job-hunt, but I list this site in a number of places in this book, for a number of reasons. In this case, if you need to research a subject—history, science, engineering, health—this is a great place to go. In the middle of the page, you'll see Subject Gateways, with links to various subjects. Unless you have some time on your hands, don't go here if you have even the smallest amount of curiosity about the world around you. There is *so* much good stuff, you will probably be wandering for a while.

U.S. Patent & Trademark Office
`www.uspto.gov/patft`

Huge databases containing trademark information and patent data going back to 1790. As with many UnderWeb locations, the site is spare and utilitarian, and you may need a little time to feel comfortable here.

Delphion $$
`www.delphion.com`

As you know, I don't usually recommend fee-based services on the Internet, but if you need to do patent searches and other intellectual property research the world over, this is hard to beat. The database is huge, the search tools extensive, the quality of data excellent. It's not cheap—unlimited access is currently $210 per month—but the data here may be worth it for you.

ARTICLES ABOUT INTERNET RESEARCH

Finding Information on the Internet
`www.lib.berkeley.edu/TeachingLib/Guides/`
`Internet/FindInfo.html`

> From the library at U.C. Berkeley, this is the best single article I've found on Internet research.

The Invisible Web
`www.lib.berkeley.edu/TeachingLib/Guides/`
`Internet/InvisibleWeb.html`

> Another excellent article from the Berkeley library, which explains more about the UnderWeb and how to find resources there.

Deep Web White Paper
`http://brightplanet.com/technology/deepweb`
`.asp#Introduction`

> From BrightPlanet, this is a really good one as well. Excellent source list of references and links.

Searching the Internet: Recommended Sites and Search Techniques
`http://library.albany.edu/internet/search.html`

> Also good.

INTERNET SITES FOR JOB-HUNTING RESEARCH

Geography/Moving/Travel/Where to Live

> The traditional three secrets in real estate—location, location, location—are the secrets of a job-hunt as well. Geographic focus, whether you are looking for a job, posting your resume, or doing research, is key to your success.
>
> You can research any place you want, simply by typing its name into your favorite search engine's query line, along with any terms to help focus the search. Hit the Enter button and see what turns up. Also, try these sites:

The Best Places to Live in America
`http://money.cnn.com/best/bplive`

Want to move to a new city, town, or country place? Wonder which one is best for you? *Money* magazine's site, here, not only has the statistics, weather, housing costs, and so on, on more than twelve hundred cities around the United States, but also a wonderful interactive feature called "Find Your Best Place." You rank nine criteria by how important they are to you, and the search engine will tell you which cities (or places) fit the criteria as you ranked them. You can specify how many cities you want, and it will give you the answers with data about each place, including a "cost of living comparator" (at `http://cgi.money.cnn.com/tools/costofliving.html`) to help you figure out whether you'll be richer or poorer if you move from where you are. If you get too many choices, you can further refine it by ranking a list of sixty-three factors; however, the more factors you check, the more you risk the chance of finding out there's no place in the country like that. Wait for heaven.

CareerJournal.com
`www.careerjournal.com/salaryhiring/indicators`

Want to move primarily for the sake of finding a job, and you wonder where the unemployment is so low that finding a job should be a cinch? This site—from the *Wall Street Journal* folks—lists precisely which U.S. communities had the lowest (and highest) unemployment rates in a recent month (for June 2004, the lowest was 2.3 percent, highest was 27.6 percent—ouch!). You know enough to tell yourself that numbers alone don't show the big picture, but hey, it's a start.

And while you're in the neighborhood . . . the WSJ also sponsors the *Real Estate Journal,* which has a section on relocation at `www.realestatejournal.com/relocation`.

American Journalism Review NewsLink
`http://newslink.org/daynews.html`

Much information on a city can be gleaned from its newspaper (and it seems like this gets truer as the towns get smaller). Here you can find links to more than four thousand newspapers, grouped by city and state. The site also has listings of radio and TV stations, magazines, and international publications. An absolute gem.

Chambers of Commerce Directory
`http://clickcity.com/index2.htm`

Need to know more about a city or town? Interested in a business located in that city? Start at the chamber of commerce. Here is a good list of city/town chambers of commerce, with links to their websites and email addresses.

The Weather Channel
`www.weather.com/activities/driving`

Need to research the weather in a certain location? Want to go visit the town or city in question? You can get a driving forecast, with road conditions, special circumstances, weather at your destination, and so on. Decided to fly there? If you're flying commercial, go to `www.weather.com/activities/aviation` for destination weather, flight times, and so on. If you have a pilot's license and are flying yourself, get winds aloft, en-route weather, NOTAMs . . . or maybe you just want to know if it's going to rain at the barbecue tomorrow, or when the sun will set, or you want to see a local Doppler map. It's all here and more. Terrific site.

ZipFind Demo
`www.zipfind.net/deluxe.aspx`

ZipFind is a company that is selling zip code–oriented software. Because these folks are the wonderful people that they are, they have placed some free utilities on their site for your use. These include a utility that allows you to calculate the distance between any two zip codes; a lookup database to find the zip for any community in the U.S.; and, most usefully, I think, a utility that tells you what other towns and cities are within various distances of a certain zip code. So if your job is to be in a new city, and you want the names of some of the surrounding suburbs, this is the place to go. If you really like the utility, maybe you'll buy some of the software.

HomeFair
`www.homefair.com`

Realtor.com
`www.realtor.com`

These two sites are both sponsored by the National Association of Realtors. There is a lot of overlap between the sites, but each also has a slightly (maybe more than slightly) different emphasis.

At HomeFair, there are a number of tools for researching communities. For example, say you are moving from a small town to a job in a big city, but you like living in small towns and want to see what other communities near the new job might be to your taste. Use the Community Calculator to see what small towns are within commuting distance. The Moving Calculator helps you see the difference in taxes, insurance, and other financial factors related to moving. The Salary Calculator compares cost-of-living factors. And so on.

Realtor.com has some of the same features, but is more about finding a realtor, looking at home listings, checking out mortgage rates, and the like. You can also find information on moving, researching schools where you are moving to, renting an apartment, and more.

CHAPTER TWO

U.S. Census Bureau
`http://factfinder.census.gov/home/saff/`
`main.html?_lang=en`

Well, who knows more about what's going on in the various communities in America than the government? Okay, maybe I asked the wrong question. Anyway, this site has an *unbelievable* amount of information. Type in an address and find out more than you thought possible about the town or city, county, people, businesses, housing ... very current info, too, not just from the well-known decennial (that's every ten years, work it into a conversation and amaze your friends) census. With all of this data riding on the work the Census Bureau does, it's no wonder they get so testy when you don't fill in the forms they send out.

IDENTIFYING CAREERS

Bureau of Labor Statistics
`www.bls.gov`

What is happening in certain industries? What is the turnover for certain careers? Outlook for hiring over the next few years? Regional data? National data? Costs of employment? Demographics of the labor force? Fatalities on the job? Wages by area and occupation? International labor data? And on and on. *Anything* having to do with work that the government wants to know is here ... and trust me, they want to know *everything*. Note also the next two entries.

The Occupational Outlook Handbook
`www.bls.gov/oco`

This is the bible of occupational fields, put out by the U.S. Department of Labor, Bureau of Labor Statistics, updated every two years, and *the* place to begin, of course, in researching particular occupational fields. Here you will find descriptions of "what workers do on the job, working conditions, the training and education needed, earnings, and expected job prospects in a wide range of occupations."

O*Net OnLine
`http://online.onetcenter.org`

The cyberspace version of the *Dictionary of Occupational Titles.*

O*Net OnLine Skills Search
`http://online.onetcenter.org/skills`

Know what your skills are, but can't translate that into a job? This page will give you some guidance. Check off the skills that you have, and the site returns job titles.

Vocational Information Center
`www.khake.com/page5.html`

What a great page! Links to almost *everything*. Job market information, economic outlook, licensing authorities, and so on. Terrific.

America's Career InfoNet
`www.acinet.org`

Linked with CareerOneStop (listed under Gateways in chapter 1) and America's Job Bank (under Supersites), this is another excellent place to research occupations and career fields, using data from the U.S. Department of Labor.

Career Converter

`http://content.monstertrak.monster.com/`
`tools/careerconverter`

> A neat little utility from the Monster College Center: you input your major (or area of interest), and the utility gives you a list of possible job titles.

The Creative Group

`www.creativegroup.com/TCG/TCGJobs`

> On this page is a list of job titles in the graphic arts industry, with links to definitions for them.

ARTICLES ON IDENTIFYING CAREERS

High Earning Workers Who Don't Have a Bachelor's Degree

`http://stats.bls.gov/opub/ooq/1999/fall/`
`art02.pdf`

Top Jobs for the Future

`www.careerplanner.com/Career-Articles/`
`Top_Jobs.htm`

Top 10 Jobs for People Who …

`www.princetonreview.com/cte/articles/`
`plan/tenjobs.asp`

Ten Hottest Careers for College Grads

`www.collegeboard.com/article/`
`0,3868,4-24-0-236,00.html`

Ten Hottest Careers in Australia

`www.jobsearchexpress.com/jobsearchexpress/`
`articles/careers/ten-hottest-careers.html`

> Don't you wonder what they would name these articles if everybody had six fingers on each hand?

CareerJournal — Salary Data and Hiring Trends

`www.careerjournal.com/salaryhiring`

Salary tables and hiring data for hundreds of fields; also shows different pay levels within careers for more senior levels and more. A Salary Calculator for comparing pay levels between different areas, as well as a Salary Search: what does *this* job pay in *this* particular area? The site also displays the latest news about salaries and salary trends, in various segments of the job market, culled from the *Wall Street Journal* daily. These articles are very current and also archived for quite some time back. Excellent, like everything on this site.

The Salary Expert
`www.salaryexpert.com`

When you need the best information, you go to an expert; and if you need the best salary information, I suppose you go to the Salary Expert. Lots of stuff on the subject here, including a Salary Report for hundreds of job titles, varying by area, skill level, and experience. Also has one of the salary calculators mentioned earlier.

Salary.com
`www.salary.com`

Probably the most visited of all the salary-specific job sites; a few years ago, they were getting over two million visitors per month, and I doubt it is any fewer now. If it has to do with salaries, it's here; many other salary sites use resources from this one.

JobStar Salary Surveys
`www.jobstar.org/tools/salary/sal-surv.cfm`

One of the best lists of salary surveys on the Net; other sites claiming to have big salary surveys actually just link to this one, the mother of all salary surveys—more than three hundred of them. Before you choose a career, before you hunt for a job, before you go in for the hiring interview . . . maybe even before you start sixth grade, you should know this information!

The Real Rate Survey

`www.realrates.com/survey.htm`

On this bulletin board, "computer consultants" (very broadly defined) post what they made on their last job or contract, and where it was. You can search this completely up-to-date site by salary, location, platform, and so on. Also includes a section called "Tips and Gotchas," with short blurbs on improving your consulting business and avoiding pitfalls.

Salary Source $$

`www.salarysource.com`

If the free sites don't give you what you want, you can always pay for the info, and maybe get more up-to-date data. Salary Source offers information services starting at $19.95.

INDUSTRY RESEARCH

Once you've identified a field that interests you, you will want to get news about that field or industry, discover trends, professional pay scales, names of associations in the field, schedules of meetings or networking events, and so on. You can start with these:

CEO Express

`www.ceoexpress.com`

Links to all kinds of business resources: the financial and business industry press, international business, trade associations . . . lots of stuff here.

Yahoo! Professional Organizations

`http://dir.yahoo.com/Business_and_Economy/`
`organizations/professional`

A good way to find out more about a particular field is to go to its association, or professional organization. Many such are listed here.

Weddle's Professional Associations
`www.weddles.com/associations/index.htm`

An excellent list of professional associations, from the site of one of the masters of the job-hunt and the Web.

The Virtual Community of Associations
`www.vcanet.org/vca/assns.htm`

It seems like every industry in the entire world has a professional association. Many are listed here, with data about the association and a link to its website. Search by keyword or browse alphabetically.

Thomas Global Register: Industry and Professional Organizations
`www.tgrnet.com/main/links.asp`

At this page on the Thomas Global Register site, you will find an extensive list of trade and professional organizations.

The Career Guide to Industries
`www.bls.gov/oco/cg/home.htm`

Companion to the Occupational Outlook Handbook (see below). While the handbook looks at jobs from an occupational point of view, the Career Guide to Industries "provides information on available careers by industry, including the nature of the industry, working conditions, employment, occupations in the industry, training and advancement, earnings and benefits, employment outlook, and lists of organizations that can provide additional information." I couldn't have said it better myself.

COMPANY RESEARCH —
CONTACT INFORMATION

Next, you will want to discover what companies, organizations, or businesses are in the field you've chosen and in the geographical area where you would like to work. One of the best places to start, on or off the Internet, is always the yellow pages, and I have listed some sites that have yellow pages–type listings . . . but you should know that these are not a reproduction of the complete yellow pages phone book you have sitting on your desk. Each one is incomplete when compared with the actual, bona fide, phone-company published yellow pages. (Nor are the secondary yellow pages, published by companies *other* than your phone company under various names, anywhere near as good as the real thing.)

So keep it in mind: your phone book knows more than the Internet yellow pages do about the local businesses in your chosen category. Keep that phone book at your elbow while doing local research. The Internet will, of course, be helpful for the far away places that your phone book doesn't cover—so long as you remember that it's not going to give you a complete listing of businesses *there,* either. Start by thinking broadly, in a geographical sense, and then move on to the other tools available to you.

Yellow.com
`www.yellow.com`

This is the best of the Internet yellow pages (or white pages, for that matter). From a single form, you can search the SmartPages, Yellow.com, YP.com, DexOnline, Real Pages, and Yahoo!'s directory listings. Results are returned more consistently (and accurately) here than on any of the others that I tried. There's also a zip and area code lookup database, with links to maps, services, and so on.

You can also find people, as the site has a section for white pages lookups at `www.yellow.com/white.html`. Other pages exist for doing reverse number lookups and address searches, as well as looking for people on the Web. It's actually a little scary . . . in many cases, people I know, including elderly women, are listed with name, address, age, phone number. I can't think of a stronger argument for unlisted numbers.

Addresses.Com
`www.addresses.com`

Another excellent resource. In addition to finding people and businesses, there are reverse email and phone lookups, links to public records, and a database of mailing and email addresses for many celebrities. So if you want a job as Madonna's hairdresser . . .

SmartPages
`www.smartpages.com`

The direct link to the SmartPages. One of the best phone and address databases on the Web.

SuperPages
`www.superpages.com`

Not all that it used to be, but may still be useful.

Search Canada
`www.canada.com/search/business`

Listings for Canada. You can search by city, province, type of business, or name of business.

COMPANY RESEARCH —
BEYOND CONTACT INFORMATION

MapQuest
`www.mapquest.com`

Okay, so you know that this is the best place to go when you want driving directions between one place and another (for which the actual URL is `www.mapquest.com/directions`). But this is also one of the best places to go when you want to find out what businesses are in certain industries in a particular city. For example, to get a list of any oil refiners within fifty miles of Santa Barbara, California, just press the Business Category button, enter "oil refiners" and "santa barbara" and "ca" in the appropriate places . . . voila! Pretty neat—and of course, you can then get a map showing you how to get there. There are no "sponsored results" in the business category search returns; when you use the phone directory sites, they will often dump ads on you. MapQuest does not.

Vault
`http://vault.com/companies/searchcompanies.jsp`

A good site for locating companies; you can search using various parameters such as industry, city and state (and country), number of employees, and annual revenue.

Entry Level Employers Search
`www.collegegrad.net/employers/search/agree.asp`

From the CollegeGrad website, this is a search engine that allows you to locate employers looking for entry-level employees. The site lets you search by a number of parameters, mostly geographical. Information returned includes the person to contact at each company, which is good to know.

When searching, keep at it. The search software will work, but it also frequently returns errors; it's kinda buggy. Another approach is to go to the page at `www.collegegrad.com/employerlinks/index.shtml`; this is a list of links to entry-level employers on the Web. Info includes how many grads and new hires they plan to employ in the coming year. Pretty neat.

Business.com
`www.business.com`

An extensive directory of businesses, organized by industry, with links to their home pages. How extensive? Ten thousand public companies, forty-four thousand private companies, and fourteen thousand international companies.

Yahoo! Company Directories
`http://dir.yahoo.com/Business_and_Economy/`
`Directories/Companies`

Another large directory, organized by industry—thousands of companies with links to their home pages.

LaborLinks
`www.afscme.org/otherlnk/weblnk14.htm`

A good page, with many links to articles and resources for researching companies. There is also a good selection of links for researching nonprofits.

EmplawyerNet
`www.emplawyernet.com`

The site has a directory of legal recruiters and employers around the country, grouped by city and state.

MORE SPECIFIC COMPANY RESEARCH

Once you know the name of an organization or company that looks interesting, you'll of course want to be able to research it, finding out as much as you possibly can, before you ever go there for an interview.

Competitive Intelligence—Get Smart!
`www.fastcompany.com/online/14/`
`intelligence.html`

This is an introductory article, written to describe what people in business can learn about rivals by skimming the Net—but for job-hunters, the most helpful parts are those that tell you how to find out more about companies that interest you.

Chambers of Commerce Directory
`http://clickcity.com/index2.htm`

As well as information on living conditions, a city's chamber of commerce often has good information about the business climate there, as well as data on various businesses and local professional associations. Go to this page for a list of chambers, with website and email addresses.

Whois.Net
`www.whois.net`

Alldomains.com
`www.alldomains.com`

If you know the URL for the company website, then go to one of these two sites (each works better in certain situations), and punch it into the site's search engine. It will look through the database of domain registrations and return basic data about the company, usually including an "administrative contact." If it's a large company, the administrative contact may be the same as the technical contact, which may be just an information technology manager or a trusted programmer in the IT department . . . but for smaller companies, you may have just gotten the name and contact info for the head guy, or close to it.

When you get your search results from Alldomains, ignore any message saying "This domain is taken"—of *course,* it's taken; you knew that. The data you want is in the scrollable box at page center. For some domain returns, you have to scroll past the "terms of use" cautions to get to the data you want.

Note that Whois.*Net* is not the same as Whois.*com.* The *net* site I have listed here allows you to do more extensive searching than the *com* site. Besides standard domain searches, you can do searches on a person's name, or find all domains that use a certain word in their URL. Note for Mac users: you may encounter problems using the *net* site.

ThomasNet
`www.thomasnet.com/home.html`

This is the website of the *Thomas Register,* the manufacturer's bible. The site is a great place to do company research. When you want to know what companies are working in what fields, there is no other resource like the *Thomas Register.* This website allows you to find basic company data, such as contact information, number of employees, parent company, and so forth. But the Internet version of the *Thomas Register* doesn't have anywhere *near* the data of the actual published version. When you are researching a company, you really should go down to the library and locate the real *Register.*

Thomas Global Register
`www.tgrnet.com`

What the *Thomas Register* does for the U.S., the *Global Register* does for the world—but even the *Global Register*'s database is pretty U.S.-centric, so if you don't find what you want at the (nonglobal) *Thomas Register* site, come here. You can search by product or company name, or browse the many industries and products listed by category. You have to register to use the site, but all the basic stuff is free.

Bizjournals
`www.bizjournals.com/search.html`

This site gathers together publications from the business press from all over the country. You can search the archive for any mention of the company (or industry or person) that you are interested in; there's a lot here. You must register, but access is free. There are other "goodies" on this site as well.

Refdesk.com
`www.refdesk.com/paper.html`

You will be amazed at how much industry and company information you can get from the newspaper—and very little of it will be available through the normal search engines. To access this data, you need to go the websites of the newspapers themselves;

the newspapers that service a company's local area are particularly valuable. Refdesk—an amazing site—has a page here that links to newspapers in every state and around the world. There is tons of information in Refdesk's archive, and even more at the websites of the newspapers themselves. Also, take a look at the Quick Reference resources at `www.refdesk.com/instant.html`.

Securities and Exchange Commission
`www.sec.gov`

All public corporations, domestic and foreign, who do business in the United States are required to file all kinds of forms and papers with the SEC. All such filings, and more, end up in the SEC's EDGAR database (which stands for Electronic Data Gathering, Analysis, and Retrieval). EDGAR is huge; and it can take a little while to get the hang of using it effectively, but what a tremendous resource.

SEDAR
`www.sedar.com`

The Canadian equivalent of EDGAR, this is a database of filings by publicly traded companies operating on Canadian soil.

Hoovers (free and $$)
`www.hoovers.com/free`

Major competitor to Dun and Bradstreet, Hoovers offers some free resources on its site. Geared toward publicly held companies, it has thousands—*thousands*—of companies listed on the site, with company officers, sales, growth numbers, employees (remember, we're still talking free here), major competitors, news, and data about the industry that the company works in. More specific stuff, like biographies of officers, annual reports, and so on, are for subscribers only, but the free stuff is still wonderful. This is a great place to start researching a company or series of companies.

Yahoo! Finance
`http://finance.yahoo.com/search`

Enter company name, stock symbol, and so on, and get back a profile of the company. Or, if you want to find companies with a word in their name, enter that word, and all companies in the database with that word in their name will be listed. (Not fool-proof, but this is one way to find companies in a certain industry: for example, enter "finance," or "aircraft," and every company that uses that word in its name will come up.) There are lots of companies in the database, and many ways of getting to them, though it will take a little exploring for you to find them all.

WetFeet Company Profiles
`www.wetfeet.com/research/companies.asp`

A directory of companies, organized by industry. Not the most complete listing available, but for the companies that *are* listed, you'll find profiles with sales data, number of employees, office locations, company and industry overviews, and so on.

4,000 Companies
`http://interbiznet.com/hunt/companies`

From Interbiznet, a listing of the Web pages of four thousand different companies.

The Virtual Chase
`www.virtualchase.com/coinfo/step1.htm`

Tons of links to resources for researching companies in various industries. When you are stuck and need an idea of how to mine company info, browse through this list.

BuildFind
`www.buildfind.com`

This is a site for researching firms in the construction industry. You can search by company, product, project, or person.

UBC: Researching Private Companies
`http://toby.library.ubc.ca/subjects/`
`subjpage2.cfm?id=273`

This is a great page from the University of British Columbia, useful for researching Canadian companies, with links to many resources.

Europages
`www.europages.com`

A basic listing of companies in Europe—five hundred and fifty thousand of them, in thirty-three countries. Not much depth to the actual company data, but the ability to browse by industry or to search for companies with *this* many employees, in *these* countries, working in *this* field, is very handy.

The Wall Street Journal $$
`www.wsj.com`

Maybe you've heard of these guys? The website is as good as the newspaper, with many links to resources for company research. You need to subscribe to really get the full benefit of the site; I don't recommend too many websites that charge for their services, but if I was job-hunting in the corporate world, this is one I would strongly consider. The cost is $79 per year or $39 if you already subscribe to the paper. As I write, there is a free two-week trial, no obligation, as well.

Note that if you subscribe to the online WSJ, your searches at Factiva (see below) are free, though there is still a documents charge for search results.

LexisNexis $$
`www.lexisnexis.com`

Factiva $$
`www.factiva.com`

Dialog $$
`www.dialog.com`

LexisNexis, the venerable search company, is not free, and if you do a lot of research here, you can run up quite a bill. But it has one of the best research databases around, as do the other two listed here. If you are not finding what you need through free services, then you might consider using LexisNexis.

Professional researchers often use the two other fee services, Factiva and Dialog, along with LexisNexis. I personally think that before you jump from free services to fee services, you should stop and see what your contacts and a little networking can dig up. Not only is this often cheaper—maybe a few lunch bills, versus nudging up against the limits on your credit cards—but it also gives you the opportunity to turn off that confounded machine and poke your head out, blinking myopically, to spend some time in the real world.

Dun and Bradstreet $$
`www.dnb.com`

The king of business report companies does not have much for free on its site, but it does have basic company contact info (for free info on the Web, Hoover's tends to be better). If you want to dig deeper into a company, then D&B sells reports, with the price listed for each company report available on the site.

ABOUT COMPANY RESEARCH . . .

Other than just identifying companies in your preferred area and industry (and maybe knowing the address so you can show up for the job interview), why should you research companies you are interested in?

- First of all, you may be able to identify problems that a company has and that your skills can solve. Identify the person with the power to hire, explain to them why *you* are in their best interests, and you may find yourself employed. The depth of research this requires is often beyond what you can get sitting at your computer, but you can at least get the basics, as well as identify your next steps, through intelligent research on the Net.

- If you have a job interview, learning all that you can about that organization reassures the interviewer that you cared enough to learn about the company before coming in for the interview. This involves research at its most basic level—the company's primary business, address, number of employees, and so on. And the Internet is good at this basic sort of research.

- You are also researching a company in order to protect yourself from making a horrible mistake—taking a job that you'll soon have to quit because of something that you didn't know or didn't bother to find out before you started there. The purpose of this sort of research is to find these time bombs *before* you agree to take the job.

In such a case, what do you want to know? Well, think of the jobs you've had in the past, and try to recall the moment when you were about to leave that job—your decision or theirs. What was it, at that moment, you wished you had known before you took the job? This will give you your research topics. Items that suggest themselves are such things as:

- What the real goals of the place were, instead of the puffery the company put in its annual report.

- What the corporate culture was like, there: cold and clammy or warm and appreciative.

- What time lines the company conducted its work under and whether they were flexible or inflexible.

- What the job was really like.

- Whether the skills you care the most about in yourself were really employed. Or was all that talk about "your skills" just window dressing to lure you there—and you, with your rich people skills, ended up spending your time pushing paper?

- What the boss was like to work for. Ditto for your immediate supervisor(s).

- What your coworkers were like: easy to get along with or difficult? And who was which?

- How close the company or organization was to having to lay off people, or how tight your department's budget was.

So if those were the questions in your past, then they are also the questions for your future. If an organization interests you, these are the things you will want to research before you get a job offer there, if you get a job offer there.

Can the Internet help with this kind of research? It depends on how deep you want to go, and, in some cases, how much money you want to spend—but spending money is no guarantee that you will find out all you want to know. Face it: there's only so much the Internet can do. If you're going to go deeper, and find out the information you really want to know, you're going to need to supplement this online research with some offline research—meaning you'll have to go talk to people, using your contacts, to thoroughly research the companies that interest you. More on people in chapter 3.

SELF-EMPLOYED AND HOME BUSINESS

Some people are just happier working for themselves, even if the hours are long and the pay is short. Try these sites for more on self-employment:

Business Owner's Toolkit
www.toolkit.cch.com/BOToC.asp

Yikes, but there is a lot of information here for the small business owner. Everything about your business: starting, planning, financing, marketing, hiring, managing, getting government contracts, taxes . . . all that stuff.

Small Business Administration
www.sba.gov

The SBA was established to help start, manage, and grow small businesses (bear in mind that it defines "small business" as one with less than five hundred employees; it could be called the

"Almost All Businesses Administration"). Lots of useful stuff here; also, check out the Starting a Business resources at `www.sba` `.gov/starting_business/index.html`.

The Business Owner's Idea Café
`http://businessownersideacafe.com`

Great site for the small business owner.

Startup Journal
`www.startupjournal.com`

The *Wall Street Journal* brings its considerable resources to bear on this site for the entrepreneur. Many articles, how-tos, advice, and resources for the business owner.

Free Agent Nation
`www.fastcompany.com/online/12/freeagent.html`

The workplace is changing dramatically. Among these changes is the fact that for some, self-employment has become a broader concept than it was in another age. The concept (for some) now includes not only those who own their own business but also free agents: independent contractors who work for several clients; temps and contract employees who work each day through temporary agencies; limited-time-frame workers who work only for a set time, as on a project, then move on to another company; consultants; and so on. This is a fascinating article to help you decide if you want to be part of this trend, on the site of the popular magazine *Fast Company.*

Working Solo
`www.workingsolo.com`
`www.workingsolo.com/resources/resources.html`

Working Solo is a good site for the home or small business worker. The best stuff on this site is at the second URL.

A Home-Based Business Online
`www.ahbbo.com`
`www.ahbbo.com/articles.html`

When they say "A Home-Based Business Online," they don't mean "An Online Home-Based Business," or "A Home-Based Online Business"; they mean, "Hey, we've got a lot of information on businesses you can run from your home, and we've put it all online for you."

Now that *that's* clear, I can tell you that this is a great site, with lots of information for you if you want to get information about a home-based business. Online. I don't mean a home-based on-line business; I mean . . . oh, never mind. There are over a hundred articles at the second URL, all about you-know-what.

Nolo Law Center for Small Business
`www.nolo.com/lawcenter/index.cfm/catID/`
`19B45DBF-E85F-4A3D-950E3E07E32851A7`

Nolo Press publishes a lot of do-it-yourself law books; this is the part of its website that offers legal resources for the small business person. Really good.

Entrepreneur.com
`www.entrepreneurmag.com`

Entrepreneur magazine's website. It has lists of home-based businesses, startup ideas, how to raise money, shoestring start-ups, small business myths, a franchise and business opportunity site-seeing guide, and a lot more. As I write, you are allowed access to the magazine's archives, with full text of many articles, stretching back to January of 1997. (This complete, no-fee archive access is unusual for most magazines.) Many resources and articles for the self-employed, home businesses, franchises . . . cool stuff.

World Wide Web Tax
`www.wwwebtax.com/miscellaneous/`
`self_employment_tax.htm`

Wow. One of the banes of being self-employed is dealing with taxes; this site has more than thirteen hundred pages to help you handle all of that. Articles, resources, links, downloadable tax forms (going back ten years!) in PDF files . . . of course, the site is selling something (e-filing tax returns), but it has a lot of good, free information about what self-employed people have to do vis-à-vis taxes, in the United States, at least.

AARP
`www.aarp.org`

In past editions of this book, I have listed AARP's small business center . . . which is no longer there. But I didn't want to just yank this well-known organization's website out of these listings, because there is still *lots* of stuff for the small businessperson—it just isn't in one single place that I can direct you to. Best bet is to do a site search on whatever you want to know ("small business resources" works well; try others), because there are hundreds of articles and useful links on this site; they just aren't organized particularly well at the time I write this. (Remember, this is the Internet; if you don't like something, just check back tomorrow; it'll be different. Works if you *like* something, too.)

Jobs and Moms: Work at Home
`www.jobsandmoms.com/work_at_home.html`

Another article on a popular women's site.

Work at Home Schemes
`www.geocities.com/freehomebasedbusiness/`
`bbb2.htm`

Not everyone using the Internet is as nice as you and I; there are even people in the world who might try to take advantage of a trusting nature. Here is an article to help you protect yourself.

Work at Home Schemes Now Peddled Online
`www.bbb.org/alerts/article.asp?ID=205`

A short article from the Better Business Bureau.

For the most part, I don't advocate people applying for temp jobs through the Internet; you will likely have better luck by going, in person, to your local agency such as Kelly, Manpower, and so on. To find your local agencies, use JobSeek (see below), or go to MapQuest (`www.mapquest.com`) and type "temp agency" under Business Category.

But as I said, "for the most part." It's not like a *rule* or anything. Here are some sites and articles related to temporary, part-time, and contract work:

The Contract Employee's Handbook

`www.cehandbook.com/cehandbook/htmlpages/ceh_main.html`

This is an immensely useful handbook, covering every facet of doing temporary or contract work. The site also has a contract employee's newsletter. It's sponsored by the Professional Association of Contract Employees.

Temp Jobs

`http://jobsearch.about.com/od/tempjobs`

From `About.com`, there are links here to articles about finding temp work, whether it's right for you, and so on.

JobSeek

`www.staffingtoday.net/jobseek/index.html`

Best way to find a temp agency on the Internet. Indicate your area, the kind of work you want, and it kicks back a list—sometimes a very *extensive* list—of temp agencies near you.

SnagAJob

`www.snagajob.com`

Part-time, restaurant, hourly, summer jobs . . . listings, resources, guidance, advice. Youth oriented, but not exclusively.

Net Temps
`www.nettemps.com`

"The Hire Power" (Groan). Hey, *they* said it, not me. I'd be tempted to list this site just for the bad pun, but this is actually a pretty good site. Advice on resume writing and such; also a jobs database.

ContractJobHunter
`www.cjhunter.com/dcsf/view`
`_some.html?SearchType=complete`

A *huge* listing of firms that hire consultants and contract employees.

Backdoorjobs.com
`www.backdoorjobs.com`

This site (and the book, by Michael Landes, from which the site takes its title) is mostly aimed at young people who are looking for summer situations, temporary jobs, maybe something out-doors, maybe something overseas for a little while . . . jobs are listed, and there is a sampling of advice from Landes's excellent book, *The Back Door Guide to Short-Term Job Adventures* (published by Ten Speed Press). Basically, the author wants you to buy his book (and it's a good book), but even so, there's a lot of useful information and news of opportunities online here.

Summerjobs.com
`www.summerjobs.com/jobSeekers/resources/`
`links.html`

This is the links page at Summerjobs.com. There are a number of really useful resources here, including Travel and Adventure, Immigration and Visas, and job sites for overseas and resort employment.

**A Professional Advisor's Guide to
Working with Nonprofit Organizations**
www.pgdc.com/usa/item/?itemID=223724

An extensive and informative article.

Careers in Nonprofits
www.bc.edu/offices/careers/careers/
careerfields/nonprofits

From the website of Boston College, this is the best page I have found on the Web dealing with this subject; great resources, good links.

GuideStar: The National Database of Nonprofit Organizations
www.guidestar.org

First stop if you're looking to identify prospective nonprofits to work for. Though the site offers fee-based services as well, you may access its database at the GuideStar EZ level for free, where there is at least basic data on over a million U.S. nonprofit organizations.

Idealist—Action without Borders
www.idealist.org

This site has some wonderful lists, categorized by field, state, and country (the directory is worldwide, covering 120 countries). It also lists other nonprofit directories that are on the Web.

Nonprofit Organizations: About.com
http://nonprofit.about.com

About.com's list of nonprofits.

LaborLinks
www.afscme.org/otherlnk/weblnk14.htm

About halfway down the page, there is a good selection of resources for researching nonprofits.

The Foundation Center

`http://fdncenter.org/searchzone`

Lists and links to nonprofits with a Web presence.

ExecSearches.com

`www.execsearches.com/exec/default.asp`

ExecSearches is a specialty job site; one of those specialties is placing people in jobs at nonprofit organizations.

The Nonprofit Career Network $$

`www.nonprofitcareer.com`

One way to go if you are looking for a career in the nonprofit sector or are looking to further the same. The site charges $40 to list your resume for one year, which maybe says something about its confidence in resumes producing quick hires. There are other resources here as well; for instance, a list of nonprofit organizations . . . not the largest database around. Still, worth checking out.

WORK FOR MINORITIES

IMDiversity

`www.imdiversity.com`

The best of the sites for minorities. Besides the standard resume- and job-posting facilities, the site is divided into "villages," with resources and articles of special interest for African Americans, Native Americans, Hispanic Americans, Asian Americans, women, and other minorities. The Career Center page is well done, and there is much here that is of value to anyone, regardless of ancestry.

LatPro

`www.latpro.com/USER/resources/links.php`

From this highly regarded site, which bills itself as "the essential Job Board for Hispanic and bilingual professionals," comes one of the best resource links pages to be found on an Internet job site, regardless of focus. Many of the links lead to Hispanic resources in the United States, as well as Central and South America. For those who are thinking of relocating outside the U.S. into the Spanish-speaking world, there are links to education and job-hunting resources, as well as networking and newspaper sites.

HireDiversity.com
www.hirediversity.com

This is a job- and resume-posting site that caters to those interested in encouraging racial diversity in the workplace.

Job Hunting after 35
www.stc.org/intercom/PDFs/2002/
20020708_20-22.pdf

It's not that the elderly are a minority, exactly; there sure seems to be a lot of them. But if any group is routinely discriminated against in the job-hunt more, with less thought, I don't know who that is. (You might argue African Americans or Hispanics, but try being an *old* African American or Hispanic.) There are not many resources for the elderly when job-hunting, though this article offers the standard advice that is pretty much echoed by everyone else. I *was* a little upset to find that the keyword *elderly* in a standard Google search kicked back an article about job-hunting after age thirty-five.

WORK FOR WOMEN

WWWomen
www.wwwomen.com

WWWomen calls itself "the premier search directory for women online." It has all kinds of resources: women's resources, women's studies, child support help, resources for single parents, mailing lists, and discussion forums (chat rooms). Under the Business heading, it has a huge list of women's associations and women's sites—the largest, in fact, that I've seen on the Web.

Femina

`www.femina.com/femina/`
`BusinessandFinance/Careers/index.phtml`

Lists "female-friendly sites on the Web." Links to a wide variety of sites of interest to women; this is Femina's careers page, with a pretty impressive list of career-related links.

Jobs and Moms

`www.jobsandmoms.com`

Resources for the working mother.

Advancing Women

`www.advancingwomen.com`

This is an international business and career site, dealing with networking, strategy, and employment for women who are looking for a new or better job, or ways to advance their career. Features chat rooms and other resources. Allied with CareerBuilder.

Job Seeking Skills for People with Disabilities
`www.csun.edu/~sp20558/dis/shcontents.html`

A virtual booklet on job-hunting for the disabled, from the Career Center at Cal State Northridge.

Jobs for the Disabled at Careers.Org
`www.careers.org/topic/01_jobs_55.html`

A *very* good list of links for job-hunters with disabilities.

Job Accommodation Network
`http://janweb.icdi.wvu.edu`

From the U.S. Department of Labor, JAN is "a free consulting service designed to increase the employability of people with disabilities."

recruitABILITY
`www.recruit-ability.com`

recruitABILITY is a resume- and job-posting service, specifically targeted toward the disabled and employers who are sensitive to their needs. The service is free to both job-hunter and employer.

Disability and the Workplace: An Internet Primer
`www.ilr.cornell.edu/library/subjectGuides/disabilityAndTheWorkplace.html`

An excellent article/link set from the Cornell University Library.

Work Support
`http://worksupport.com/Topics/employment.asp`

This is a website with "information, resources, and research about work and disability issues." The page I have provided at the site has an article titled "Job Applicants and the ADA" (the ADA is the Americans with Disabilities Act) and links to more articles about employment issues for the disabled. The site has other resources as well.

WORKink
www.workink.com

> A Canadian site designed for job-hunters with disabilities, with job- and resume-posting services and other resources. It has extensive—and current—listings of jobs for the disabled; access is, of course, free.

Closing the Gap
www.closingthegap.com/index.lasso

> A site about the use of information technology to help the disabled in the workplace.

WORK IN EDUCATION

Search for Public Schools
http://nces.ed.gov/ccd/schoolsearch

Search for Private Schools
http://nces.ed.gov/surveys/pss/
privateschoolsearch

Search for School Districts
http://nces.ed.gov/ccd/districtsearch

> Provided by the National Center for Education Statistics, these three databases of schools and districts around the United States is absolutely indispensable if you are looking for a job in K–12 education. You can search using various degrees of specificity; for example, you can look for all schools within twenty miles of a zip code. Data returned includes contact info, student count and ethnic mix, other schools in the area, and on and on. Free and *very* helpful.

Academic Info
www.academicinfo.net/studentcolleges.html

Although the site is not always the prettiest to look at, and you need to poke around a little to find what you are looking for, there is an *extensive* list of colleges and universities here, organized by state. Although intended as a guide for students, this same information is helpful when job-hunting in secondary education; it seems to me that a lab assistant doesn't want to waste her time at a school that doesn't have a laboratory, nor does a professor of astronomy want to teach at a school without an astronomy program.

As I said, it may take a little work, but this site has a lot to offer. For more than the list of colleges and universities, go to the home page at www.academicinfo.net and see what you can dig up.

American School Directory $$
www.asd.com

I'm kind of breaking a rule of mine here, in that I don't like to recommend a site that is fee based unless it offers significant free resources . . . but if you are looking for a teaching job, for a $36 yearly subscription fee (or $9.95 for a one-month trial), you get access to a database of over 100,000 school districts in the U.S. If the National Center for Education Statistics sites don't yield enough results, you *might* want to consider this site. Along with contact information, the Web address, and the number of students and homerooms, there are "wish lists" for each school, indicating the types of teachers needed.

National Teacher Recruitment Clearinghouse
`www.recruitingteachers.org/channels/`
`clearinghouse/index.asp`

> Resources for those interested in a teaching career; there are also job listings on the site.

State Departments of Education
`www.recruitingteachers.org/channels/`
`clearinghouse/deptedu.asp`

> Also from the National Teacher Recruitment Clearinghouse, a list of each state's department of education, to help you find job data, certification information for that state, and so on.

National Directory of Women's Education and Training Programs
`www.womenwork.org/resources/directory.htm`

GRANTS

> It may be that the work you most want to do right now is not of the sort for which most companies would be willing to pay you. Perhaps you are a writer, researching a book, or an artist, sculptor, or musician. Maybe you want to run a social program for the homeless or engage in similar selfless endeavors. For those of you who are drawn to pursuits for which our society does not generally pay well, if at all, I present a list of sites where you can investigate the possibility of a grant.
>
> Now, don't think for a moment that this is easy, or a way to get through life without working, or any kind of substitute for a "real job." The chances of *ever* getting a grant are astronomically small, and it is an area where those who know the most about how to get a grant will generally come before those who are more worthy, but ignorant of the process. And, even if you *do* get the grant you are seeking, you must manage the project being funded well, account for all money to the penny, and make sure you avoid even the appearance of impropriety. A job is *way* easier.
>
> But people who are drawn to these sorts of things are usually not the types who let little things like extreme difficulty deter them, so here goes:

GrantsNet: An Electronic Roadmap for Grants
`www.hhs.gov/grantsnet/roadmap/index.html`

The federal government gives away millions of dollars every year. Unless your uncle is a U.S. Senator, your only way of getting some of this money is through the competitive grant process. That is, you write and submit a proposal, as do many, many other people, and if your proposal is judged to be one of the more worthy, you receive the money necessary to fund it. Or, more likely, nowhere near enough money to fund it—at least, not from a single source.

This is arguably the best site for accessing the widest variety of government grants. The road to a government grant is often a long and difficult route; they have chosen a good metaphor for the site. But there is a lot of information here, and it would be the first place I would go to start the process.

GrantsWeb
`www.research.sunysb.edu/research/kirby.html`

The best single website I have found for finding grant information on the Web.

Grants and Funding Information Service
`www.lib.washington.edu/gfis/resources/`
`webstuff.html`

This site, and the other sites and databases it points toward, is more academically oriented than others. There is a lot of information and links to searchable databases of funding sources.

Database of Arts Resources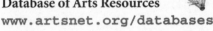
`www.artsnet.org/databases`

If you are an artist looking for funding, this is probably the first Internet resource you should turn to. Includes an excellent searchable database of funding sources.

Grants.gov

`www.grants.gov`

Partnered with the U.S. Department of Health and Human Services, this site is the only point of access, they say, for more than nine hundred grant programs. There is also much good information here on how to apply, writing a proposal, and so on.

ED.gov

`www.ed.gov/fund/landing.jhtml?src=rt`

The U.S. Department of Education will provide over $40 billion in the coming year, in the form of grants for various purposes. Most will go to school districts and educational institutions; some will go to individuals for education and training.

HUD Grants

`www.hud.gov/grants/index.cfm`

More government money; this time, from Housing and Urban Development.

National Endowment for the Arts

`http://arts.endow.gov`

You've heard of it; everyone else has, too.

SRA International

`www.srainternational.org/newweb/`
`grantsweb/index.cfm`

At the website of the Society of Research Administrators International, there is information on public and private funding sources for those in the research community.

Art Deadlines List

`www.xensei.com/users/adl`

Announcements of art grants, organized by deadline.

Art A to Z: Artist Grants
`www.antiquesatoz.com/artatoz/grant.htm`

Another good place to go if you are an artist in need of a grant to pursue your art. The site also has many resources for artists in general.

GENERAL RESEARCH

Sometimes you need to do some basic research for your job-hunt—that is, you need to find data that does not specifically relate to the next company you are going to approach, or the like. In such a case, you will need to turn toward the general research tools on the Net:

The Free Dictionary
`http://thefreedictionary.com`

Actually, it's more than just a dictionary: there's also a thesaurus, an encyclopedia, specialized dictionaries for the medical, legal, and computer fields, a literature reference library, and a search engine, all on one page.

A hint: this site is more useful once you get past the home page. Once you have it look up a word, you can then choose which of the resources you want to use to further research that word, phrase, or concept.

OneLook Dictionaries
`www.onelook.com`

Best on the Web. They have indexed at least 970 dictionaries, with more than 6,097,226 words in them. Indicate what word you want defined, or spelled, or pronounced, and it will tell you what online dictionary or dictionaries have your word. The site offers you a link to that dictionary's definition; click, you're there. OneLook lets you choose the reference you want for your definitions; since definitions of some words will vary, depending on the field you are researching, this ability to pick the reference work you want is a good one. OneLook is also good for translations and reverse meanings: for instance, "dating of tree rings" accurately brings up "dendrochronology."

Refdesk.com
www.refdesk.com

This is what you'd call a "meta-research" page; it seems like every possible Web resource is here. There is so much at this site, I can't list it all, but allow me to paint in broad strokes:

On the home page, without scrolling (what I call "above the fold"), you can do searches through Google, MSN, Refdesk's own database, or do lookups in Merriam-Webster's dictionary and thesaurus. You can catch up on the latest news, see stock quotes, and get the official time in the United States from one of the government's atomic clocks, accurate to two-tenths of a second.

As you scroll, you gain access to People Search (directory lookups); current news, both national and local (type in your zip code); reference sites; quick looks at lists such as government 800 numbers; phone numbers of your local officials; and on and on. This almost wasn't a Parachute Pick, because I hate, detest, abhor . . . hold on, let me look in the thesaurus . . . loathe, despise, and execrate pop-up ads. But if you have a pop-up blocker, or if you feel love, affection, devotion, fondness, yearning, or ardor for pop-up ads, then by all means, go for it.

Internet Public Library
www.ipl.org

Though I mentioned the IPL earlier in this chapter, under Directories, it does have more to offer, of course; part of that "more" is a reference library with links to online general and specialized reference works.

About.com
`http://azlist.about.com`

About.com is different from most of your research resources on the Net, for every entry was compiled and written by actual people, specifically for this site—in fact, almost five hundred people, writing on thousands of subjects. Excellent and authoritative. The URL I have given you is for the "A" page from the site's A to Z browser; here you can start looking through the list of topics alphabetically. At the top and bottom of the page are the links to the rest of the alphabet.

Answers.com
`www.answers.com`

This is a pretty neat general reference tool. Access to dictionaries, encyclopedias, search tools, and so on, all from a single page, with some pretty neat features. For instance, I have read a lot, since I was a kid, and have run into many expressions that I am familiar with by *sight*, but have no idea how to pronounce. An example is the term *trompe l'oeil*, which means "trick of the eye." It is used to denote a style of decoration meant to deceive, such as painting a picture directly on the wall of an open window and the scenery outside. I have never known how to pronounce it, but when you go to Answers.com and type in the term, the dictionary return has a little speaker icon. Click on it, and you hear a recording of the proper pronunciation.

But of course, it doesn't stop there. You can have Answers.com search the Web (you can direct it to Google or Yahoo!, but unguided, it searches Teoma, Jeeves, About, Overture, and Yahoo!) for references to the term; conduct an image search, and display examples of the style (there's a good one at `www.artewo.ch/g_trompeloeil/img_p1.jpg`); check through current news to see if the president has taken up painting as a hobby . . . not bad, huh? It's not world-shaking, and everything here can be done at other sites, sure, but this one does it more smoothly than most, without sending you off to other sites where you have to deal with advertising, pop-up ads, dancing vitamins, etc.

Although not as useful for direct research as it is for developing contacts, you can still get some value from newsgroups—which have nothing to do with news. Rather, these are discussion groups, kind of like chat rooms. Each is on a different subject; everyone is allowed to post whatever they want on that subject, and everyone in the world can read what has been posted. The name of the group tells you the subject under discussion.

Just like your browser (Internet Explorer, Netscape) allows you to read what's on the World Wide Web, there are specific programs for accessing the Usenet part of the Internet. They are known as "newsreaders" or "newsgroup readers" (though historically, they have been called "clients," and many Internet veterans still refer to them this way). Nowadays, some limited newsreader capability is built into versions of Explorer and Netscape.

Setting up and using a Usenet client can be a bit confusing for the novice. But you have luck on your side: a while back, Google bought up a company that had tons of newsgroup postings going all the way back to 1981; it archived and indexed all of that content. That means that you can read all of this more-than-twenty-years of data with your regular Web browser and search it, using Google, for what you are interested in.

There are about forty thousand different newsgroups, and Google has indexed and gives you access to a large number of these. Frankly, I'm not sure how many it covers. Google claims 845 million postings, using up about 600 gigabytes of storage space, which is *way* more than one person can read in a lifetime. If you find that you need more than Google has, you will have to get a newsreader like Agent or XNews.

But you won't know if you need more than Google has to offer until you try it out, so, by all means, look at what's available there:

Google Newsgroups Page
`http://groups.google.com`

I will warn you now: most of what is on Usenet is absolute tripe: people's opinions about this or that, flames (where someone is harshly ridiculed for having posted something others disagree with), bad data, old data, false data, worthless data . . . tripe. But there is *so* much stuff there, that even if only one-tenth of one percent of it is valuable information—probably just about right, proportionwise, I think—then that still means there is a *huge* amount of useful information to be had. In fact, if we take Google's figures and apply my worthwhile to worthless ratio, that still leaves about a quarter million pages of good stuff.

And that is why Google's indexing of this part of the Net is so wonderful. Being able to search through the mounds of bunk, without having to read it all, is a gift beyond measure. Heck, even being able to search through the *good* stuff without reading everything is wonderful. (You can search Usenet with a news client as well, but searching across different groups is easier with Google.)

We'll discuss Usenet and newsreaders a bit more in chapter 3; for now, here are a few places where you can learn about Usenet:

Google's Groups FAQ
`http://groups.google.com/`
`googlegroups/help.html`

Answers basic questions about Google's groups and how to access them.

Slyck's Guide to the Newsgroups
`www.slyck.com/ng.php`

A multi-page tutorial about newsgroups; some parts are a little advanced for most people. Use the Next and Previous buttons at the bottom of each page to navigate.

Beginner's Central Usenet Tutorial
`www.northernwebs.com/bc/bc40.html`

A very informative article about this part of the Net.

ibiblio's Usenet Help

`www.ibiblio.org/usenet-i/usenet-help.html`

More than anybody ever wanted to know about Usenet.

Usenet Lore

`www.searchlore.org/usenet.htm`

An intermediate to advanced guide on searching with Usenet.

BOOKS ABOUT INTERNET RESEARCH

If you could only get one book about doing research on the Internet, I would recommend that you get *Find It Online,* by Alan M. Schlein, from Facts on Demand Press, 2004. Excellent, current, authoritative, readable, and useful beyond belief, whether you are researching on the Net or writing about it.

Another that you might consider is *The Invisible Web,* by Chris Sherman and Gary Price, Information Today, Inc., 2001. Not as current as I would like, but this book is still a classic in the field.

EVALUATING THE DATA

Once you have the results from whichever search engines you use, how do you evaluate the data? I've mentioned how the Internet has leveled the playing field for everyone from the largest corporations to the smallest hoaxer. In many cases, the source of the data—whose website it is on, the newsgroup it is from, or the writer of the email—will tell you a lot about how trustworthy that data is. For cases that are less clear-cut, there are five criteria to use when evaluating data from the Net:

- Authority: *Who* put the information here? Who wrote it? Why?

- Accuracy: *How much* is verifiable? What were the writer's sources?

- Objectivity: *Why* is the material here? Who supports the site? How does the information relate to any site advertising?

- Currency: *How old* is the information? Is it datable at all?

- What does the site look like? Professional? How is the data presented? Free of tyPos and speling erorrs?

There are a number of ways you can evaluate the currency of a page, outside of the page's information itself. For example, if you use Netscape as your browser, and you are unsure of how old a page is, you can look under the View menu and choose Document Info; it will show you the date that the page was last revised. In some cases, it may be some years, and this *generally* means that the data on the page is no more recent. (There are exceptions, particularly with dynamic pages.) For pages with a security setting, you can check the date on the security certificate, using either Netscape or Internet Explorer. And if you use Gigablast as your search engine, the date that the page was last modified is usually shown; other search engines may indicate when the page was indexed.

You can find more about evaluating Web data at:

SofWeb: Using the Internet
`www.sofweb.vic.edu.au/internet/research.htm`

DISCIPLINE

One of the problems with doing your job-hunt research on the Internet (or . . . writing a book about it) is that you can find so many interesting side paths. This can easily divert you from your job-hunt or career change, for weeks, all the while giving yourself the illusion that you are hard at work: "Hey, what do you mean I'm not working very hard on my job-hunt? I spent six hours yesterday on the Net."

When doing your research on the Internet, bring loads of self-discipline. You must know exactly what it is you want to find: make a research plan, write it out on paper, and stick with it. Set yourself a time limit for your data search; don't exceed it. If you've tried to find the data on the Net, and it just isn't there, stop, and try some other methods to mine the data. If you *do* find the data you set out for, stop there as well. Naturally, your research plan will change as you chase the data and get a better idea of what can, and cannot, be found on the Internet. But make sure that all of your surfing, I mean, research, is leading you toward your goal. You're looking for a *job*, remember?

CHAPTER THREE

Contacts and Networking

Here's an interesting little tidbit: one of the most successful ways of finding a job is by picking up the phone book, calling around to the businesses listed in the fields you are interested in, and asking if they have any job openings. This method of job-hunting is listed as having a 69 percent success rate (meaning that, out of a hundred people who use *only* this method in their job-hunt, sixty-nine of them will be successful). Now, this is the interesting part: if you do *exactly* the same thing, but you do it as part of a *group* of people who are all job-hunting this way, the rate of success jumps to 84 percent.

The primary reason for this higher success rate is that the people in the group talk, and they tell each other what they each have found. *You* may not have had any luck today, but you talked to a guy who happened to mention that he is looking for someone in the same line of work as Bob, who is sitting over there near the end of the table. And of course, Bob doesn't have anything that can help *you* right now, but sitting across from Bob is Mary, and Mary just talked to a guy who knows a couple of companies that might be interested in someone like you. And so on. Had these people in the group *not* been talking with each other, their likelihood of job-hunting success would be the same as if they all had been doing it alone.

People love to talk. We are social animals. If people can't talk to each other face-to-face, then they will invent other ways to talk to each other, to wit, the telephone. And when actual talking is impractical or impossible, they will find other ways of "talking": smoke signals, telegraphy, traffic lights, graffiti, letter writing, hand signals, and sign language. And of course, people do the same thing on the Internet, using bulletin boards, email, chat rooms, Usenet groups, and websites, specifically set up for nothing but talking. And all of this works to the job-hunter's advantage.

In its essence, all job-hunting is a search not only for information but also for people—for human links between you and information, between you and a prospective employer. These days, such links are called "contacts," and a common word for all of your contacts is your "network." Not surprisingly, the act of mining this list of people for information, and for more contacts, is referred to as "networking."

In the job-hunt, networking is often the secret of the game. Consider: a 2003 study showed that for the companies participating, 60 percent of their new employees were hired through employee referrals or the Internet. Since other recent studies

have shown that the Net accounts for less than 10 percent of new hires, that leaves us with *half of the open jobs being filled through networking.*

The quickest way to find a job is when a friend tells you that they need someone exactly like you where he is currently working. Now of course, it isn't usually that easy. But if you don't *directly* know someone who can tell you of a job opening, then the next step is to see if any of your friends know of someone else, who might be aware of an opening. Or maybe one of *their* friends do. And so on, extending farther out away from you. And interestingly, the farther out you go, the more likely you are to find a job this way, and it's not just because of the increasing number of people involved.

THE STRENGTH OF WEAK TIES

It seems like a huge number to me, but the experts say that most people know 250 people. When they say that you "know" that many, they don't mean that you go out to dinner with that many, or even have the home phone number of every one of them. But that's the number of people whom you can claim as friend, relative, or acquaintance—people you interact with, who would recognize your name. Within your circle of 250, there is your *core*: the few with whom you are especially close, along with maybe another twenty or thirty that you socialize with or see regularly. Outside of your core is the rest of your 250; these are the ones that you are obviously not as close to, like your wife's brother out in Oregon, that nice older woman in the accounting department, your sister's no-good kid.

It makes sense that the people you are closest to will have more in common with you; they will tend to have the same interests as you, and they will tend to know the same people as you—there is a lot of overlap between *your* circle of 250 and *their* circle of 250. And because of that overlap, they will be more likely to know what you know. And in the same way, *they* will be less likely to know what *you* don't know—in this case, of possible job openings.

It is when you start getting farther away from your core, and start finding people with less overlap between your 250 and theirs, that you will find the people—and the information—that you and those closest to you are less likely to know. Though it seems paradoxical, it is the people that you know the *least* well who are most likely to be helpful in your job-hunt. This is called "The Strength of Weak Ties."

You cannot ignore this concept. To make your job-hunt more successful, you need to find the people you do not know well, or at all. The *less* well you know them, the *more* helpful they are likely to be to you. And, lucky you, the Internet is pretty good at this.

INTERNETWORKING

Before I show you some links to online articles about networking on the Internet, I'd like to point out that while networking is something the Internet does pretty well, there are very few good online articles about how to do it. There aren't even that many good *offline* articles about how to do it. What that says to me is that like any relatively new tool, people are still learning how to use the Net in this capacity; maybe it also says that not all people are comfortable with the whole concept of networking in general, during their job-hunt.

But even if that's true, it just means that this is an area that is ripe for innovation and new approaches. If you come up with an idea for how to do this better, that can only be to your benefit. Who knows? You might even have a new career ahead of you.

Why Networking?
`http://content.monster.com/career/`
`networking/bigdeal`

A basic networking article at Monster.com.

How to Network Like an Expert
`www.wetfeet.com/asp/article.asp`
`?aid=215&atype=Networking`

The best single networking article I have found on the Internet. If you only read one, read this one . . . but, of course, you shouldn't stop after just one.

Not Asking for Help Is Top Networking Mistake
www.findarticles.com/p/articles/mi_m1272/
is_2699_132/ai_106473709

A short but very good article about networking properly.

Networking on the Network
http://polaris.gseis.ucla.edu/pagre/
network.html

Though aimed at college students—Ph.D. students, to be precise—this rather lengthy (67,000 words!) article has some good ideas about networking. It is not the prettiest you will find on the Web, but there is a lot of helpful stuff here. All of it is good, but if you are in a hurry, skip to http://polaris.gseis .ucla.edu/pagre/network.html#section9.

Career Playbook: Job and Career Networking
www.careerplaybook.com/guide/networking.asp

Some good tips in this one.

Informational Interviewing: A Networking Tool
`www.quintcareers.com/informational`
`_interviewing.html`

Readers of *What Color Is Your Parachute?* will be familiar with the critical concept of the informational interview: meeting with someone whose interests are similar to yours and finding out what and whom they know that may assist you in your job-hunt. Quintessential Careers' website has a good series of articles on how to do this properly.

Networking Your Way to a New Job
`www.quintcareers.com/networking_guide.html`

Also from Quintessential Careers. Check the site thoroughly for more articles on this subject.

FINDING PEOPLE YOU KNOW

Networking is all about people. Some of them you know; some of them you don't—yet. Even when you know them, you won't always know exactly where they are. Here are a number of tools for finding somebody when you know who it is you are looking for (and don't forget chapter 2, which also has some good resources for finding people):

Yellow.com
`www.yellow.com/white.html`

Listed in chapter 2 as one of the best sites for looking up businesses, this is also one of the best for finding people. From a single form, you can search the WhitePages.com, Addresses.com, 411.com, InfoUSA, and Yahoo!'s directory listings. There are also pages for doing reverse number lookups and address searches, along with a search for people who have a Web presence. Also a zip and area code lookup database, with links to maps, services, and so on.

Eliyon Business People Search
`http://networking3.eliyon.com/PeopleFinder`

Pulling data from a number of resources, this site can come up with surprising results. Enter a name and you'll get a list of people and their business affiliations, sometimes going back for years (this is one instance where outdated information on the Internet can be quite valuable). Click on the name for email address and other data.

InfoSpace
`www.infospace.com`

One of the best people finders on the Net, although it works for businesses as well. In addition to having a very complete database, it boasts some neat little features. For instance, say you're going to pick some guy up at his office; where's a place nearby to grab a burger? No problem; nearby businesses are listed, complete with maps.

Addresses.com
`www.addresses.com`

Another excellent resource. In addition to finding people and businesses, there are email and reverse phone lookups and links to public records.

Langenberg.com: PeopleFinder
`http://person.langenberg.com`

From a single page, this site allows you to access a number of people-finding resources: the Verizon White Pages, email address searches through Bigfoot and Yahoo!, alumni searches, professional associations, Usenet postings, obituaries (!), and the membership lists at MSN and ICQ.

I have to say that this is a *good* site, but it is not a *great* site. It would be a *great* site if all of the links worked as they should. But during the times I have tried it, some of the page's resources worked fine, while some were painfully slow, and others just plain didn't work, period. So, if you're striking out with the other sites

I have listed here, give this one a try. Hey, this is the Internet; by tomorrow, the site could work perfectly, or it could be gone completely.

Canada 411

`www.canada.com/search/people.html`

People listings for Canada.

FINDING PEOPLE YOU DON'T KNOW

Okay, so you don't know anybody. Not a problem! The number of contacts you can make online is mind-boggling. Any faraway place that interests you, you'll likely find a contact online. Any question you need an answer to, you'll likely find someone online who knows the answer. Any organization where you need to meet the person with the power to hire, you'll likely find someone online who knows somebody who . . .

And how do you find these people? The Internet has a number of tools for doing this. Never will a single method work in all cases, but here are the basic ways of meeting people on the Net:

Chat rooms are places where you "meet with" other people, online, at the same time, and talk with each other using your keyboards. It's like watching the dialogue from a play script unfold line by line on your screen. Chat rooms are found on commercial services such as America Online and MSN; on websites such as Yahoo! Chat; and at many hundreds (if not thousands) of special-interest websites, where people can chat about that site's specific subjects. Some job-hunting sites have chat facilities.

Generally, the chat sessions will be between a number of people—most sites allow any number of people to "listen" but may limit the number of people who can get in at any moment to "talk." Some of these will be moderated, meaning that there is someone in charge, watching over the conversation, with the power to disconnect those who behave badly, but in fact, these are rare, and most sites require self-policing. Many sites allow you to search through past conversations by keyword, so be careful what you say; it may be stored somewhere for a very, very long time. Some chat sites will allow you to leave the main thread and "go off" to a private room for one-to-one conversations, but these are usually sites that lean toward personal relationships rather than business ones. In fact, of all of the ways you can meet and communicate with people, chat rooms are the *least* likely to be useful in your job-hunt.

Message boards—which, more and more these days, are being called "forums"—are similar to chat rooms, except that the conversations do not occur in real time. They are more common than chat rooms and, for job-hunting purposes, *far* more useful—in fact, they can be absolute gold mines. They are found most often at websites devoted to a particular subject, field of interest, or function, such as magazines, industry or hobby sites, career sites, colleges, and so forth.

All *forums* will have a general subject or field of interest, usually related to the subject of the hosting website. For example, Ezine Articles is a website for writers; you can go to its message board at **www.ezinearticles.com/forums**. People use this area to discuss various aspects of writing.

Different parts of the forum are divided into subheadings within the field. You can think of these like rooms in a house, where each room is dedicated to a specific area of the larger subject. So, here, there are rooms labeled Self-Publishing Tools and Resources, Where Else to Promote Your Articles, E-Book Tools and Resources, Ghostwriting Questions and Answers, and so on. Anyone interested in one of these more specific subheadings can click on the title for access to that "room."

Once a person is in the room, he can read previous conversations—called "threads"—or start a thread by asking a question or making a statement for discussion. Anyone can read any thread, and those registered with the site (which is almost always free) can post a response to any thread. The response—officially called a *reply*, gee, there's a surprise—can occur almost instantaneously, or it might be years later, and all replies become a part of that particular thread. The thread itself belongs to, and stays in, the same subheading, or room, where it was started.

Some threads "die" without any replies, or very few. Some threads generate multiple replies, replies to replies, and so on, and the thread can go on and on, sometimes for weeks or months. At any time, multiple threads are active, and in theory, *all* threads started since the birth of the board are active, though in practice, threads do tend to die after a while from lack of attention. All threads, active or not, are always searchable, by subject, keyword, date of posting, name of person who posted, and so on. Which is to say, *everything* that has *ever* been said on this board is searchable, and accessible by anyone, *forever.* As a practical matter, you should limit your searches to specific time periods. If you go too far back in your search, you run the risk of outdated information, as well as data overload.

One of the things that you will notice if you spend much time on message boards/forums is that certain people tend to post more often than others, and that others' replies to them will tend to be extra respectful and deferential. These are the people you should cultivate; they tend to be authorities. They know a lot about their subject, and they seem to know the most other people. If you want to communicate with one of these people only, most message boards will allow you to send messages directly to that particular person; these are called *private messages,* or PMs. Private messages are *not* included in the board's database and are not searchable or viewable by others. This is how people exchange email addresses without exposing themselves to spammer harvesting bots and the general nuisances that sometimes hang around the boards. If you spend time on message boards and get to know the people there, they can be *terrific* places for cultivating contacts.

Newsgroups are very similar to message boards, except that while message boards are always found on the Web, newsgroups are from a part of the Internet that predates the Web, called Usenet. (In fact, just to be technical, Usenet is not a *part* of the Internet, but it is accessible *through* the Internet.) Originally, newsgroups were used to spread news about their subjects; now, there is no pretense of such a limitation, and you can find all kinds of things discussed and posted here.

Not all Internet service providers will give you Usenet access, and not all ISPs give you access to all of the possible groups. But

Google has archived a large number (they claim thirty-six thousand) of the available newsgroups and continues to do so. You can search and access these through your Web browser, regardless of whether or not your ISP allows you Usenet access.

Usenet group names look like this: alt.subject.subheading. If you look at the parts of the name, separated by dots (golly, we used to call those "periods"), you'll see that it's a *hierarchy,* meaning the name starts out generally descriptive and gets more precise as you read from left to right, just like a website URL. With Usenet, they all start with a prefix, which gives you the general area—the *very* general area—of the group's subject of interest. There are thousands of hierarchies and group prefixes. Here are some of the more common ones:

alt.   this used to mean *alternative,* as in "an alternative approach to" whatever-the-subject-in-the-rest-of-the-name-is. This was back in the days when the Internet was full of college kids and society's young rebels. Now, it more or less means "this group is about anything," because yesterday's rebels are today's mainstream.

rec.   subjects dealing with recreation

comp. computer related

sci.   science

soc.   social and societal areas

net.   network or Internet related

For a complete list of all Usenet name hierarchies, go to `www.magma.ca/~leisen/mlnh/mlnhtables.html`.

All newsgroups are open to everyone with Usenet access. Since it dates from the early days of the Internet, Usenet remains a favorite part of the Net for those people who know more about computers and the Internet than most of us; we might unkindly call them geeks or hackers. Newsgroup postings are in text only, and they lack the pretty formatting that you are used to seeing on the Web (as well as some of the message boards' abilities, like private messaging).

Overall, I would say that newsgroups are more likely to produce contacts and job-hunting information for academics or those in the information technology fields. If you are not in one of these areas, you may well do better to stay away from Usenet and stick with the other possibilities the Net has to offer.

Networking websites are sites specifically set up for networking. Examples are LinkedIn, Friendster, ICQ, Tribe, WorldWIT, and Monster Networking. Each is a bit different from the others, but all have been set up in acknowledgment of the power of networking in business (and other) relationships, and job-hunting certainly not the least of these.

Mailing lists are similar to newsgroups but are done through email, and they don't always carry the varied threads that Usenet groups do. Mailing lists exist on every subject possible; you subscribe to the lists you want to receive by sending an email; those lists are then sent to you periodically. If you want to stop subscribing, you send an "unsubscribe" message. (The subscription process is completely automated; I once had a heck of a time getting off some lists when the underlying software was incorrectly installed by the list manager, because there was no human to contact.) Like Usenet, mailing lists are another older Internet device. Many lists, at least the noncommercial ones, are disappearing. There are just better ways of communicating on the Net these days.

Compared to message boards and Usenet, mailing lists are a slow method of communicating, particularly for the job-hunter. Though at times useful for gathering information, they are not as immediate in their nature as the other possibilities on the Net, so I would not recommend them for direct communication with others. But still, hear me well, dear reader:

Every resource on the Internet (and off) can always be used for contact/data mining and name gathering. Who are the authorities in the field? Who is it that others listen to? Who is respected and well known? What people write the bulk of the articles and periodicals in the field? Who are the people that others interview most? Quote most?

Generally, the people who are more highly placed in their field will be the ones who know the most people in their field; as a corollary to "The Strength of Weak Ties" principle, the people that *they* know well will also tend to be more highly placed.

These people will, of course, tend to be busier than most, but they are no less approachable for that. Just remember that anyone

you contact on the Internet (or off) should be approached respectfully, politely, courteously, with keen awareness on your part that this is a busy person who may or may not be able to respond to you. If they do help you, email thank-you notes should always be sent to them, promptly (within three days) for the help they gave you.

CHAT ROOMS

Yahoo! Chat
`http://chat.yahoo.com`

Still the king of the chat room, Yahoo! has hosted chat groups for years, and thousands of people have used Yahoo! to increase the reach of their personal networks. Because it is so well known, it is one of the first places I would go for general chat subjects.

WetFeet
`www.wetfeet.com/discuss/home.asp`

WetFeet is one of the better job-hunting sites, and they have a good selection of job-oriented chat rooms on the site.

AOL and MSN

If you have either of these services, they both have extensive chat and messaging areas.

Before I list places for you to go to access message boards, I should mention that in almost every case, the entries here would be second on my list of places to go. I think you are far more likely to make useful contacts at forums that are specifically related to the industry or field of interest that you are targeting for your job-hunt; these forums will normally be found on the websites of industry magazines, associations, or even large companies in that field. Generally, you can locate these by using your favorite search engines and searching on something like "[name of industry] forum," "[subject] message board," or "[field of interest] discussion group"; use your imagination. Also, try searching lists of periodicals and industry magazines and newsletters, and then checking their websites.

If that doesn't bring results, then you can try some of these:

Monster
`http://network.monster.com/Community.aspx`

Once you register with Monster, you can go to the Boards area of the Networking pages (see Monster Networking below). Currently, there are thirty-three different boards grouped under General Interest, Special Interest, and Industry Focus, to meet others in your target industry.

Yahoo! Groups
`http://groups.yahoo.com`

They do everything else, why not this? Yahoo! has thousands of groups: industries, hobbies, personals, careers . . . tons. If you look under Business and Finance, many of the groups you will find were created for networking in specific industries.

Note that Google Groups and Yahoo! Groups are not the same thing. Google Groups are Usenet newsgroups, while Yahoo! Groups are closer to standard message boards, though there are some specific features that are unique to Yahoo! And just to confuse things further, Google Groups 2 (see next entry) is a beta feature that is very much like Yahoo! Groups.

Google Groups 2
`http://groups-beta.google.com`

As an adjunct to its Usenet database, Google is starting a Message Board/Mailing List service. The content of this will eventually be added to the current Usenet database. This feature is currently in beta testing, which means that Google hasn't completely worked out all the bugs, but feel free to use it (and report any flaws you find in the software). You can search the existing groups or start a new one.

CareerJournal Discussion
`http://discussions.careerjournal.com`

CareerJournal, the career site sponsored by the *Wall Street Journal*, has a discussion area on its site. In some ways, it's a little different than most forums; email addresses are required and posted, and some subjects are topical and not permanently kept open. I generally advise against posting your email address for all to see; you can check what's on the site and make your own decision.

HotJobs Communities
`www.hotjobs.com/htdocs/client/splash/communities`

This is from Yahoo!'s career site; there are thirty-five industry-specific message boards accessible here.

Tribe
www.tribe.net

There's more about Tribe below, under Networking Websites; but for now, you should know that Tribe is a place where you sign up, get your friends to sign up, and so on, and form communities called "tribes." You can then use the resultant contacts to look for a job, buy a car, find a roommate, and so on. Tribe also has a message forum, where you can talk with people who have similar interests and goals.

Delphi
www.delphiforums.com

A general forum site, which claims 4.5 million users in more than 100,000 groups. How nice.

NEWSGROUPS

Google Newsgroups Page
http://groups.google.com

Probably the best place to go these days for finding newsgroups. The index is very easy to browse, the database is very searchable, and it claims to have over a trillion postings.

If I may repeat what I said in chapter 2, most of what is available on Usenet is absolute tripe: people's opinions about this or that, flames (where someone is harshly ridiculed for having posted something others disagree with), bad data, old data, false data, worthless data . . . tripe. But we are looking for people now, not valid data. You will be able to apply your own sense of truth to what you read, and you will soon know who knows their stuff, and who doesn't. If you aren't clear about which is which (or who is who), try another part of the Net, where there is less data smog.

Google's Groups FAQ
`http://groups.google.com/`
`googlegroups/help.html`

If you are unfamiliar with Usenet and/or Google, this will answer your basic questions about Google's groups and how to access them.

Tile.Net
`http://tile.net/news`

I happen to love Tile.Net; I list it in a number of places. No frills, nothing fancy, just *lots* of listings in various categories—in this case, thousands of newsgroups, organized by description, hierarchy, or name index. The Description category will usually be best for discovering groups, the Index when you know the group name you want. Clicking on a group takes you to a summary page; many of these summaries contain links to Web or FTP documents where you can learn more about the subject and, of course, who wrote it. Aha, an authority! Not a bad place to start.

Clicking on the group from the summary page will cause your newsreader client to come up . . . if you have one installed. If you have Microsoft Office, then Outlook can function as a client . . . but I would recommend Agent or Xnews myself. If you don't want to worry about setting up a client, use Tile.Net to locate the newsgroup you want, and then see if Google has it archived.

Newsgroups: Beginner's Central
`www.northernwebs.com/bc/bc40.html`

If you want to know more about Usenet newsgroups and how to use a Usenet client, this page is excellent. It assumes you know almost nothing and goes on from there. The page link I have given is one where clients in particular are described, but if you navigate the site a little, you'll find lots of stuff on all aspects of the subject. In fact, if there is *anything* you want to know about the Internet and how to use it—email, browsers, the Web, FTP, even Telnet—it's all here, complete and very well written. The index is at `www.northernwebs.com/bc/index.html`.

MAILING LISTS

Topica

`http://lists.topica.com/dir/?cid=0`

On this website is a list of mailing lists for oodles of subjects; lots of newsletters are mixed in here, too. Not all of them are going to be useful, of course, but with a little work, you will know which ones are going to bear fruit as you are looking for contacts.

Tile.Net

`http://tile.net/lists`

Again, not a fancy site by any means, but one of the most useful sites on the Internet. This is a list of mailing lists, organized by name, description, and domain; you will find Description most useful.

L-Soft CataList
`www.lsoft.com/lists/listref.html`

Access to more than seven-two thousand mailing lists, searchable by keyword, country of origin, and so forth.

NETWORKING WEBSITES

I love invention and innovation. Much of the dot-com boom and bust was (in my opinion) because would-be entrepreneurs didn't really innovate; they just tried to use the Internet as another avenue toward services that were already available offline. Very few Internet-based companies have been successful using this strategy.

The companies that *have* been successful on the Internet are the ones for which there is no offline equivalent; eBay is a perfect example. There wasn't a huge preexisting need or a problem crying loudly for solution, but eBay is arguably one of the most impressive of the Internet success stories. A solution before there is a problem: now *that's* innovation.

I doubt that they can achieve the financial success of eBay, but the networking sites that have been created in the last few years are also excellent examples of innovation, for which there is no real offline equivalent (at least at this scale). In acknowledgment of the power of the networking concept, people are now using these intertwined networks of computers—the Internet—to increase the power of the *real* networks behind them: the people at those computers.

Other than the online dating sites (I kind of see these as the Internet being a solution for the isolation it helps to create), the next most popular sites for connecting people are the business and job-hunting network sites. Here is a sampling of some:

LinkedIn
www.linkedin.com

LinkedIn is nothing less than an *excellent* business network site. In form, it is similar to the others; in implementation, superior. When you sign up (registration is free), you enter your basic information—field, job title, geographic area, and so on—and indicate what kind of connections you are looking for and what kind of incoming contacts you are willing to accept. For example, if you currently own a business, you could indicate that you are open to inquiries about employment at your business, but naturally you don't want people sending you job offers for yourself.

You then go on to invite people to enter your network—you cannot draw people in unless they actively want to be included. As the people that you know join, and the people *they* know join, your network grows. At LinkedIn, your network is defined as a maximum of four levels, or degrees, out to a friend of a friend of a friend of a friend. For example, if only five people join at each level, that is still a network of 625 people. In reality, it is likely to be far more.

LinkedIn also allows you to contact people who are not in your network, if they have said they are willing to accept such contacts (and naturally, you may allow such contacts, as well). Currently, LinkedIn has more than 74,000 such people. Anecdotally, the most connected person on the site has a network of 3,677 people. More than 50,000 of LinkedIn's registrants consider themselves job-hunters, even if their current employers do not.

Tribe

www.tribe.net

Tribe is very similar to LinkedIn, but takes a larger worldview. Why limit your network contacts to just business? What about if you needed to buy a used car—would you rather buy from a stranger or from a friend of a friend? If you were looking for a roommate, would you rather run a newspaper ad or find candidates among your network? If you needed a new dentist, whose recommendation would you trust?

This is what Tribe is about. As with other networking sites, you invite people to join, you have easy access out to four degrees, and so on. But at Tribe, your network—of course, here it is called your "tribe"—can be used for many purposes. Job-hunting is, of course, included, and the site even has job postings. But you also can use your tribe for buying and selling, housing, recommendations, special interests, and so on. There are even messaging forums, for common interest discussions among registrants.

Tribe, and its many uses, does bring up an important point: this is all about *trust*. When you are inviting people to join your tribe, you should only invite the people you know well, and trust. If a friend that you invited into your tribe sells another friend a used car with a blown engine, it's going to come back on *you*. The people you invite in are counting on your recommendation that *all* of the people you have invited to join are trustworthy, and so it goes, out through all *your* degrees and into *other* people's. Don't invite your sister's no-good kid, just to pad the numbers.

In fact, this applies to *all* of the networking sites. When you invite someone into your network, you are inviting them into not just *your* network but the networks of the hundreds and thousands of people who connect to you. These people are all—*every one of them*—depending on *your* judgment about those you have invited, just as you are depending on theirs. The system collapses if the people involved are not truthful, reliable, consistent, and principled.

WorldWIT
www.worldwit.org/Default.aspx

Women, Insights, Technology (WIT) is the basis for this women's networking organization. With more than thirty thousand members, it offers more than just an online presence; the group consists of more than seventy chapters in the United States, Canada, and worldwide, organized by geographic area (AustinWIT, IowaWIT, ItalyWIT), with local events supported as well as online connections.

Friendster
www.friendster.com

Friendster is not intended for business relationships; it is really more of a friendship and dating site. But when you are job-hunting, I think that you should leave no stone unturned. This should certainly not be your first stop, but with a claimed member base of more than five million people, neither is it a resource to be blithely ignored. On Friendster, you can search for friends who might already be members, invite new ones, send private messages, and visit discussion forums.

Monster Networking
http://content.monster.com/network

The well-known job site has recently started a networking area. You post your profile, indicate the kind of people you want to hook up with, search for other Monster networkers by skills, company, interests, and occupation. Honestly, I still think there are a few bugs to work out on this portion of the site. Though meant for business, it has a bit of a dating feel to it—why would I upload my photo for a potential business relationship? The message boards in the networking area are not well policed, either; there were stay-at-home-and-make-a-fortune-with-your-computer type ads posted when I last was there. But Monster is a pretty good company. I anticipate it will get this right, in time, so if you've already signed up with Monster, check the networking area every now and then.

Networking for Professionals (possible $$)
`www.networkingforprofessionals.com`

Networking for Professionals is a little bit different from the standard networking model. You don't "invite" people you already know to help you form a network; NFP is a site for when you want to meet people that you *don't* already know, people that your network might not otherwise lead you to. Everyone who signs up here, is here to meet people they otherwise would probably *not* find.

When you sign up, you enter your personal information and can post a resume; then you indicate what sort of business relationships you are interested in cultivating. You can also search the database of members to find professionals in certain fields.

The first month of membership is free, and you will receive a free month for every person you convince to sign up; also, people outside the New York City region are eligible for free memberships. If you have absolutely no connections to anyone or find that your network has dead-ended for your present purposes, you might consider coming here.

Tools for Career Networking
`www.quintcareers.com/Internet_networking`
`_sources.html#online_communities`

An excellent list of various networking resources available on the Internet.

Networking Services Meta List
`http://socialsoftware.weblogsinc.com/`
`entry/9817137581524458`

Here you will find lists of hundreds of networking sites: business networking, common interest networking, dating, meeting facilitation sites. Very extensive.

Networking Resources by State
`www.job-hunt.org/job-search-networking/`
`job-search-networking.shtml`

Job-Hunt has a list here of links to networking resources, organized by state.

Guide to Online Networks

`www.onlinebusinessnetworks.com/`
`online-social-networks-guide`

This page, from the Online Business Networks website, has summaries and full reviews of a number of business networking sites.

LatPro

`www.latpro.com/USER/resources/links.php`

LatPro is a job board for Latin and Hispanic professionals. Here, on its Resources page, are some links to sites that can help with networking during your job-hunt.

BuildFind

`www.buildfind.com/buildfind.jsp`
`?tab=People&query=`

This is a search engine whose database is confined to the construction industry. If you are looking for someone who works as an executive in architecture or construction, this is the first place to go.

A WORD OF ADVICE

There are many, many networking sites, and competition is fierce. Friendster says it's going to start adding job-hunting resources, Google recently jumped in with its orkut site, Tickle claims eighteen million (?!?) members . . . *and not one of these sites is connected to any other*. The resulting networks are completely isolated.

Surveys show that people who register at these sites tend to visit often at first, but then the visits trail off, becoming more and more infrequent. It's fun at first, but who has the time to nurture hundreds of relationships?

My advice is to visit many, see which ones you like, and then register with one or two, *maybe* three at the most—certainly no more—and stick with those. At some point, even online, quality of relationships has to supercede quantity.

Also, though your immediate goal is to find a job, don't stop nurturing these relationships just because you've found employment. The people who helped *you* will, in turn, need *your* help one day. And you may find yourself job-hunting again in the not-so-distant future; no one will appreciate it if you only turn up on their virtual doorstep when *you* are in need.

A CATEGORY ALL ITS OWN

craigslist
`www.craigslist.org`

Craigslist describes itself as an "online community"; it's a good description. Originally started in the San Francisco Bay Area, craigslist has quickly grown into a series of websites in forty-eight U.S. cities, as well as in cities in Canada, the United Kingdom, Ireland, and Australia. The site is nothing special to look at, but the minimalist approach fits it well; craigslist is about function and getting the job done. Style is *not* the point. Instead, you come here to look for a job, sell your dishwasher or buy a car, find where to catch some live music this weekend, join in discussion groups on a variety of subjects, find an apartment or meet that special person, register to vote . . . it is an online reflection of the places where we live. A community.

More particularly, and somewhat redundantly, there is the "community" section (the site, you'll notice, doesn't really believe in uppercase letters), which is a series of running forums on different subjects. You can use this community section to hook up with people in the same line of work, start a job club, look for investors for your new business, and so on; almost anything goes. Another section allows you to post, and look for, "gigs," which are typically one-day (or less) jobs. If you are still job-hunting when the savings run out and need to pick up some short-term work—as well as look for something more permanent *and* make connections with people that can help—then craigslist is the place to go.

MISCELLANY

Alldomains.com
`www.alldomains.com`

Maybe you don't know anybody at the company you are interested in, and you can't seem to come up with a contact there at all. Assuming the company has a website, you can, as a kind of last resort, plug the company's website URL into Alldomains's search engine. It looks through the database of domain registrations and returns basic data about the company, usually including an "administrative contact." If it's a large company, the administrative contact may be the same as the technical contact, which may be just an IT manager or a trusted programmer in the IT department . . . but for smaller companies, you may have just gotten the name and contact info for the head guy, or somebody close to him.

When you get your search results, ignore the message about "This domain is taken"—of *course* it's taken, you knew that. The data you want is in the scrollable box at page center. For some domain returns, you have to scroll past the "terms of use" cautions to get to the data you want.

Whois.Net
`www.whois.net`

Similar to Alldomains, sometimes Whois works better. Note that Whois.*Net* is different from Whois.*com*. Whois.Net has more features.

Weddle's Professional Associations
`www.weddles.com/associations/business.htm`

Where are you likely to find those who are doing what you want to do? This is a terrific list of professional associations, from the site of one of the masters of the job-hunt and the Web.

PEOPLE AT THEIR BUSINESS

If you need to locate someone's business, or their business's website, try these next few entries:

Vault

`http://vault.com/companies/searchcompanies.jsp`

A good site for locating companies; you can do a search using various parameters such as industry, city and state (and country), number of employees, and annual revenue.

Business.com

`www.business.com`

A pretty extensive directory of businesses, organized by industry, with links to their home pages. How extensive? Ten thousand public companies, forty-four thousand private companies, and fourteen thousand international companies.

Yahoo! Company Directories

`http://dir.yahoo.com/Business_and_`
`Economy/Directories/Companies`

Another extensive directory, organized by industry—thousands of companies with links to their home pages.

If you need more tools than these to uncover specific companies, to help you locate the person or persons you are looking for, turn to chapter 2. Many of the places listed there are excellent sources for finding contacts. For example, a number of the business directories list contact information for people at thousands of companies. On the Internet, it is rare to find a single route to the person or information you are looking for.

BLOGS

Short for "Web log," a blog is a website that functions as a kind of daily diary for someone with a website. The site owner can write about whatever he or she was thinking about that day, what happened to them, and what they did. Many blogs have links to useful Net sites that their writers have found.

Most blogs have some sort of theme. Some, in fact, have themes that center around job-hunting and networking, and you could mount a convincing argument that blogs *themselves* are a form of networking.

As you can imagine, if the person writing the blog is smart, witty, bright, and (this part is important) writes well, it can be very entertaining and even occasionally helpful in your job-hunt. These, however, are few in number.

If you are interested in the concept, there is a comprehensive list of blogs at CyberJournalist: `www.cyberjournalist.net/cyberjournalists.php`.

EMAIL

We cannot talk about contacts on the Internet without discussing the main method of communication on the Internet. How well—or how badly—you use email can have a serious effect on your ability to bring your job-hunt to a successful conclusion.

From the employer's point of view, job-hunting is not so much a process of *selection* as it is a process of *elimination. This* person has spelling errors on her resume, *this* person never finished his degree, *this* person hasn't returned my calls . . . the pile of applications, or resumes, gets thinner and thinner.

When you are job-hunting online, the primary impression that people have of you is from your emails with them. If you dash off quick notes with sentence fragments, spelling errors, and poor grammar, you may never get to make an impression on them in person. Use email as a way of getting your communication to a person quickly, but don't let that sense of speed and efficiency slop over into the way you write.

Thank-You Notes

If someone does you a favor, email them a thank-you note within twenty-four hours, or as soon after that as is practical. In special cases, you might consider sending them, in addition, *another* thank-you note by regular mail, through the U.S. Post Office. (You wouldn't believe how many letters I have received, telling me that thank-you notes were the one thing that made the difference in someone's job-hunt.)

Note that prospective employers, people you would like to add to your network . . . in fact, *anyone* you want to make a good impression on during your job-hunt, may not get the impression of you that you want if you have an email name like "sexykitten2" or "12packbob." Your ISP will usually rent you extra email addresses for dirt cheap. You don't have to get rid of your current "fun sounding" email address; just get an additional one for your job-hunt, with a name that sounds more businesslike.

Additionally, when using email:

- Take the time to learn how to use at least the basic features of your email client: do you know how to send and receive email attachments? Use the address book? Set the spam filters? You should learn how to use these features *before* you need to.

- When sending email, send it as plain text; don't send emails with HTML formatting, fancy fonts, colored text. The person receiving your email may not be using the same email program as you, may not have the same features, or may have their options set differently. As a consequence, your emails may look like gibberish when received. If you must send formatted text, send it as an attachment to an email, using a standard word processing program like Microsoft Word (though don't send email attachments unless they are requested). Always explain in the body of the email what the attachment is.

- Make sure the subject line is short, pithy, and accurate. It doesn't hurt to repeat the subject line as a "re:" at the top of the email text.

Resumes and Email

According to jobs-and-Internet expert Peter Weddle, fully half of all employers now prefer to receive resumes online. Should you send it as an attachment to an email, so it retains its nice look, or send it in the body of an email, even though it probably looks far less attractive that way?

The experts say that you should only send your resume as an attachment to an email *when you are specifically requested to do so by the prospective employer*. Most employers will not accept email attachments, period, as a security precaution. You don't want your email and attached resume to be filtered out and thrown away before it reaches the person you sent it to. That means that you will need one version to use as an email attachment or hard copy, and another version that you can paste into an email.

So, using your preferred word processing program (Word, Wordperfect, and so on), you should prepare an attractive resume, making sure that it looks as professional as possible. This is the version you will send through the postal service or add as an attachment to an email when one is requested.

Next, copy the text and paste it into a text processor, like Windows' Notepad or the Mac's SimpleText. This will strip it of the extra formatting commands that the word processor embeds in the file. Format this text version of your resume so that it looks as nice as plain text can look, and save it under a different file name (or with the ".txt" extension instead of ".doc"). This will be the email version of your resume. Vary the margins to change the line length and see what it will look like on different screens and email clients; make the changes you think necessary so that it will look best under the widest variety of conditions. When you send your resume by email, this is what you will paste into the email body.

Finally, Martin Kimeldorf suggests adding something like this to the end of your email resume: "An attractive and fully formatted hard copy version of this document is available upon request."

Security and Spam

During the course of your job-hunt, you will be exchanging emails with many people you don't know well, or at all. Email is more likely to infect you with a computer virus than anything else you'll do with your computer during your job-hunt, and accidentally infecting someone else could affect your chance of receiving a job offer from that person. So, remember the standard warnings:

- *Never* respond to an unsolicited commercial pitch; don't even "opt out" from a mailing list you didn't ask to be on. Usually, this will only confirm your email address as a good one.

- *Never* give out passwords, credit card numbers, and so on, in response to what may look like a legitimate message from your bank, credit card company, ISP, eBay, Paypal, and so on. They will *never* ask you to do this; anyone that does is a crook masquerading as your bank or other service, hoping to get your passwords and credit card numbers.

- *Never* even click on a link in an unsolicited email (this can infect you with a virus, or automatically load a program onto your computer that spies on you).

- *Never* click on or open a program sent to you by email that you didn't ask for. Again, this can plant a spy on your computer that records your keystrokes and sends them to a hacker so he can cull out passwords and personal data.

- Never open a "security software patch" or anything similar, sent unsolicited from what appears to be Microsoft or another software company. Don't even click on a *link*, even if it appears to indicate that it's at Microsoft or another legitimate company; it's not. Again, this is a spy program.

I use Eudora and Netscape when I am on the Net, which are not Microsoft programs. This is partly from long-standing habit, and partly for security reasons. Since most people use Microsoft programs, those are the programs that hackers target when they are exploiting software security weaknesses (and all programs have such defects, regardless of manufacturer). No matter what programs you choose to use, make sure that you have antivirus software installed, active and current.

Spam—unwanted email advertisements—are, these days, just a fact of Internet life we have to accept. The Can-Spam Act is a joke, and until the government actually comes up with a solution (I myself favor a tenth of a cent fee for every email sent), there is nothing you can do about it.

Spammers have crawler programs, just like search engines do, that prowl the Internet looking for email addresses. Most of the addresses are no good, some are good, and the spammer doesn't know which is which. Until, that is, you click on that "opt-out" link at the bottom of the email, and tell him your email address. Ah, *now* he knows he's got a good one.

And it doesn't matter that the spammer has to send out ten thousand emails to get one sale, or even a bite. Most of the offers are bogus, anyway; he just wants your credit card number, with no intention of delivering goods for payment.

Most of the current solutions to spam are problematic for the job-hunter. Some spam-blocking programs won't let you accept emails that aren't from people in your address book, but since you'll be getting lots of emails from people you don't know while you are networking and job-hunting, using such a program won't work. Other programs send the email back to the sender, and make the person send it again. How's *that* for annoying? Forget that one.

No, as things are right now, the best you can do is just set the filters in your email client to catch surefire spammer words, most of which I cannot list here in a family book, and minimize the chances of them getting your email address in the first place. This means not posting your email address where the crawlers are most likely to find it, like Usenet and message boards.

And, if you *do* have to post your email in these places for some reason, try this: if your address is tomsmith@hotmail.com, you can type it as "tomsmith-at-hotmail.com." Most people will know to replace the "-at-" part with the "@" sign, but most spam crawlers will cruise right past it. (If you think the people you are corresponding with are not that Net-savvy, add instructions for them to include the "@" sign.)

Here are a few links to help you use email more effectively:

Email Netiquette
`www.library.yale.edu/training/netiquette`

From Yale University; short but very good. A must-read for every job-hunter.

Email Etiquette
`www.emailreplies.com/#15formatting`

Though written as a set of rules for formulating email replies to customers, most of it applies to all email communications.

Avoiding Spam
`http://cexx.org/spam.htm`

The best site I have seen on the subject. Another must-read.

A Beginner's Guide to Effective Email
`www.webfoot.com/advice/email.top.html`

Not necessarily for beginners; there are many good tips here for everybody, regardless of experience level.

Email Cautions
`www.freewarehof.org/email.html`

A humorous approach, no less valuable for that.

CHAPTER FOUR

Counseling and Testing

At some point, you may realize you need a little career counseling, perhaps some skills testing, and you're hoping to find these on the Internet. Naturally, the Internet cannot replace a live, face-to-face career counselor. But the Internet can give you quite a bit of guidance for your job-hunt.

As usual when on the Net, you must exercise caution. I am stupefied at some of the superficial (and just plain wrong) advice that I sometimes read online about job-hunting, resumes, and the like. But, that small objection aside, all that you would hope for is available: tests, articles, manuals, FAQs. The whole works.

ONLINE TESTS: PERSONALITY/TRAITS

The interactive tests available online fall into two categories: personality tests and career or vocational tests, though sometimes the line between them gets a bit hazy. The majority of the personality tests/games/instruments online will yield results that indicate your personality "type." Clearly, this is not the same as a career test, but as *Chicago Tribune* columnist Carol Kleiman once pointed out, it is important that your future job or career fit your personality, so, "personality" is not without career *implications*, at the very least.

In my view, though, the fundamental defect of personality-type instruments is that they are great at illuminating the *style*

with which you do any job, but they are often misguided at predicting what career(s) that implies. I can tell you from decades of experience: dream jobs or careers are defined by much more than "type" or "style." I would therefore take all personality-type career suggestions with a huge grain of salt. But they can stimulate your own ideas, which is always a good thing; for that reason alone, these tests may be worth taking.

Some of these instruments, particularly the Myers-Briggs Type Indicator (MBTI), are much loved by many career counselors. Note that the actual Myers-Briggs Type Indicator is not offered for free on the Internet. But other tests, quizzes, or sorters dealing with personality type are:

The Keirsey Temperament Sorter
www.keirsey.com

Author David Keirsey categorizes people by temperament, and it is possible that through a more complete understanding of your temperament, you might find more insight into the type of work that is best for you.

This somewhat complex website has lengthy descriptions of the various temperaments, as well as links to the Keirsey Temperament Sorter, which is available in several languages besides English, ranging from Spanish and German to Japanese and Ukrainian. The site is interactive, and once you've answered its questions, it gives its results to you in Myers-Briggs-Personality-Type language ("you are an ENFP")—with colored graphs. As I said, it is a rather complex site, and you will need to spend a little time here to fully understand what the test is telling you, but stick with it if you think it worthwhile.

The Enneagram Institute
`www.enneagraminstitute.com/Tests_Battery.asp`

The Riso-Hudson Enneagram Type Indicator (RHETI) is another personality test, with the results grouping you among nine basic personality types. Though popular as personality tests go, how much it has to say about career choice is debatable. But we can say this much: career choice is always a search for the self, and for work more fitting to that self. In this sense, the Enneagram, like other tests of this sort, at the very least has career implications, and is useful for stimulating self-awareness, self-observation, and growth.

This is the "official" Enneagram site; any other websites with the test will be licensing it from this site, so it has some authority. The URL indicated has a couple of versions of the Enneagram test (and others), ranging from free sample tests to the full Enneagram test, which takes forty minutes and costs $10.

The RHETI Test
`www.9types.com/homepage.actual.html`
`www.9types.com/rheti/homepage.actual.html`

Another Enneagram site. The first URL is the site's home page, which has some explanation of the nine types, a link to another version of the RHETI test available on the site, plus links to other Enneagram and personality-type pages. The actual test is found at the second URL listed; it is a "sample" Enneagram test, in that it has 38 of the normal 144 questions found on the full RHETI.

The Enneagram: An Adventure in Self-Discovery
`www.ennea.com`

For those who want to do further research into the whole idea of the Enneagram, here you will find a very complete list of Enneagram resources, seminars, history, and so on. You will notice that the site is a member of the Enneagram WebRing: WebRings are virtual circles of like-minded websites, where you successively click on Next, Previous, or Random links to get to the next site in the Ring.

ColorQuiz
`http://colorquiz.com`

Why do people tend to buy the brands of sugar that have blue on the package? Why do so many institutions have pink walls? Color evidently has a lot to do with human personality and motivation. Based on the famous work of Dr. Max Luscher, this simple test takes five minutes, is free, and is different from most personality tests in that all you do is click on colors. Note: The test didn't work with Netscape, but did work correctly with Internet Explorer.

The Classic IQ Test
`http://web.tickle.com/tests/uiq/`
`authorize/register.jsp?url=/tests/uiq/`
`index.jsp`

Probably the best free IQ test available on the Web; you may have seen it as you've clicked around, at a wide variety of sites linked to Tickle. You can take the test, and get your basic score, for free. More detailed results are available for a price (which is $12.95 at the moment), *but* you'll get signed up for a "subscription," an unfortunately common marketing gimmick these days.

HumanMetrics: Jung Typology
`www.humanmetrics.com/cgi-win/JTypes2.htm`

A free test, based on the Myers-Briggs.

Myers-Briggs Type Indicator $$

`www.discoveryourpersonality.com/MBTI`

If you feel that you absolutely *must* take the genuine MBTI to get on with your job-hunt, and you have $60 to spare, then here's one place to find it. More test resources, and testing sites, may be found at the Myers-Briggs Foundation website at `www.myersbriggs.org`.

Google: Tests and Testing

`http://directory.google.com/Top/Science/`
`Social_Sciences/Psychology/Tests_and_Testing`

If you find the above-listed resources insufficient, then take a look at Google's testing page. There are many, many links to testing sites available on the Web. Some are free, some are not. Some are *way* not. Use good judgment, especially if you test low in that area.

Working Out Your Myers-Briggs Type

`www.teamtechnology.co.uk/tt/`
`t-articl/mb-simpl.htm`

Though they want to sell you a form of the MBTI here (current cost is about $265 U.S.), you can go to this page if you are interested in reading about Myers-Briggs Type testing. A really good article.

Resource Materials on Personality Types

`www.ibiblio.org/personality/faq-mbti.html`

If you want to learn more about personality types than is available online, the ibiblio site has an extensive bibliography of printed materials that you can look for in your local library or bookstore.

ONLINE TESTS: CAREERS

We turn now from personality tests to career tests, also called vocational tests. Before you look at these, you should familiarize yourself with the Five (unless I think of more) Rules about Taking Online Career Tests:

No test can measure *you*; it can only describe the family to which you belong. Tests tend to divide the population into what we might call groups, or tribes, or families—namely, all those people who answered the test the same way you did. It all comes out as: "You are an ISFJ." Or, "You are an SAE," or, "You are a 'Blue.'" The results are an accurate description of that tribe, that family of people, in general, but they may or may not be true in every respect of *you*. So when you see your test results, keep in mind that these are the test results for the defined group that answered the questions the same way you did. As you can see by looking at the various tests, the number of groups, and how they are defined, can seem a bit arbitrary. You may be exactly like that group, or you may be different in important ways.

Don't predetermine how you want the test to come out. Stay loose and open to new ideas. It's easy to have an emotional investment that the test should come out a certain way. I remember one time I was administering a test about geographical preferences in the United States, where job-hunters had to prioritize a number of factors, and then decide which of the states these pointed to. One woman was long-delayed in arriving at an answer, so I asked her if she was running into any problems. She said, "No, I'm just prioritizing it. And . . . I'm gonna keep on prioritizing it, until it comes out *Texas!*"

You're looking for clues, hunches, or suggestions, rather than for a definitive picture that tells you exactly what you should do with your life. "A lightbulb going off, over my head" is how some people describe what they got out of taking a test—at the most. If your goal in taking such a test, or series of tests, is that you're just looking for lightbulbs, you will enjoy these tests much more.

Take several tests, not just one. One may send you horribly down the wrong path. Three different tests can offer a more balanced picture or a more balanced set of clues. An online test isn't likely to be as insightful as one administered by a qualified psychologist or counselor, who may see things that you don't.

Finally, don't try to force your favorite online tests on your friends. You may take a particular test, think it's the best thing since the invention of the wheel, and try to "sell" it to everyone you meet. Don't. Just because it worked well for you does not

mean it will work well for them. If you ignore this, your friends will start running when they see you coming.

As a corollary to this, it might be fun to talk with your friends about the results of qualitative tests, but do *not* compare scores for quantitative tests; the IQ test is a classic example. One person's score will always be higher; it's not a situation that brings out the best human qualities.

That said, on to the tests:

The Princeton Review Career Quiz
`www.princetonreview.com/cte/quiz/`
`default.asp?menuID=0&careers=6`

A twenty-four-question quiz, related to the Birkman Method (a test, like the MBTI, that is only available on the Internet for a fee). This one, however, is free, and may have some good suggestions for you.

John Holland's Self-Directed Search $$
`www.self-directed-search.com`

My favorite career system for many years has been John Holland's RIASEC system and its stepchild, your three-letter Holland Code, which you determine by taking his Self-Directed Search instrument. You can take the official test here, and receive your results for $9.95. Though not officially sanctioned, there are similar tests available for free; see the following entries.

The Career Interests Game
`www.career.missouri.edu/modules.php?name=News`
`&file=article&sid=146`

Many years ago, in a playful moment, I invented a brief, quick, hazy overview of Holland's RIASEC system, based on the idea of someone walking into a room where a party was going on. My idea was that different groups (the Holland RIASEC groups) were gathered in six separate corners of the room. It's called "The Party Exercise," and here is a simplified version of it online, at the University of Missouri site. Here it's called "The Career Interests Game," and while the exercise lacks the central graphic I originally had, the site has otherwise done a good job of presenting it in color, with career links and so on. It gives you a good first guess at your three-letter Holland Code.

The Career Key

`www.careerkey.org/english/you`

This test also does well in giving you your three-letter Holland Code. There are many useful links on the site, as well as information on occupations that match your code.

Holland Themes: Sample Self-Assessment

`www.soicc.state.nc.us/SOICC/`
`planning/c1a.htm`

Another approach to finding your Holland Code.

Career Briefs

`www.soicc.state.nc.us/SOICC/`
`info/briefs.htm`

This is a listing of occupations and descriptions; the Holland Codes for each occupation are included, so if you have taken any of the tests here, or otherwise have some idea of your code, then some browsing through this site can give you some ideas for careers.

HotJobs Career Tests

`http://hotjobs.careerid.com/articles.html`

There are three basic tests here that may give you some career guidance.

CareerPlanner.com $$

`www.careerplanner.com`

CareerPlanner has a Holland-type test on this page; it will cost you from $19.95 to $29.95, depending on how fast you want your results back. If you click on the link that says, "If you decide not to buy right now, click here," you may be taken to its page at `www.careerplanner.com/Career-Test-Career-Search/Discount25.cfm`, which will give you a 25 percent discount. The discount may not be there by the time you try it, but hey, that's the Internet.

The Career Values Test
`www.stewartcoopercoon.com/jobsearch/`
`career-values`

A quick way of identifying the things you value most in a career, from the mind of well-known job expert Dick Knowdell.

Top Jobs Matching Your Interests and Needs
`www.princetonreview.com/cte/articles/`
`plan/tenjobs.asp`

If you want some ideas for possible careers or jobs, you will find lists here like, "The Top Ten Jobs for People Who Can't Stand Ties or Pantyhose," or "The Top Ten Jobs for People Who Like to Work with Their Hands" . . . like that.

Highest Paying Jobs
`www.resumagic.com/highestpayingjobs.html`

Lists of the jobs with the highest salaries (national averages, of course) for no college education and for two-year, four-year, and graduate degrees.

The Best and the Worst
`www.careerjournal.com/jobhunting/`
`change/20020507-lee.html`

In this brief article from the *Wall Street Journal* site, you'll find links to lists of the "ten best" and the "ten worst" jobs in America.

A Guide to Going Online for Self-Assessment Tools
`www.careerjournal.com/jobhunting/`
`usingnet/20030429-dikel.html`

Also from the WSJ site, this article by jobs expert Margaret Dikel.

TRANSFERABLE SKILLS

Readers of *What Color Is Your Parachute?*—that's all of you, right?—are familiar with the concept of transferable skills: essentially, that you are defined not by your job title, but by the skills that you possess, which are transferable from, and to, any occupation you may happen to be involved in at the moment. It will come as no surprise to you that there are transferable skills tests available on the Internet:

Transferable Skills Survey
`www.d.umn.edu/student/loon/car/`
`self/career_transfer_survey.html`

From the University of Minnesota, a quick online test of your transferable skills. Test results will show you your strongest and weakest areas.

Skills Search
`http://online.onetcenter.org/skills`

From O*Net OnLine, this quick test will help you link your skills to possible occupations, using the U.S. Department of Labor's database. Once identified, you can look at lots of current information about these, including salary level, hiring rates, and so on.

Motivated Skills Test
`www.stewartcoopercoon.com/jobsearch/`
`freejobsearchtests.phtml`

Some experts say that it is not your transferable skills that matter, but the ones you most enjoy using. They call these "motivated skills," or "key skills." On this site is a test you can take, to help you find your motivated skills.

Assessing Your Skills and Accomplishments
`www.uwrf.edu/ccs/assessskills.htm`

A good article from the University of Wisconsin website.

Transferable Skills

`www.quintcareers.com/transferable_skills.html`

From Quintessential Careers, an article series that details the concept of transferable skills, with lists of skills and advice about how to emphasize these in your resumes and cover letters.

JOB-HUNTING: ONLINE GUIDES

There are online job-hunting manuals everywhere on the Web. Their general quality has increased enormously since I first published this book, but the first two still stand out:

Creative Job Search

`www.deed.state.mn.us/cjs/cjsbook/index.htm`

This site, maintained by Minnesota's Department of Employment and Economic Development, has put together the equivalent of a job-search manual. A superior example of the breed.

Career Development eManual

`www.cdm.uwaterloo.ca`

Here is another excellent guide—they call it an eManual—from the Career Center at the University of Waterloo in Ontario, Canada. Its self-assessment section is one of the best on the Internet; naturally, the links throughout the site tend to be Canada-centric.

CollegeGrad.com Job Search

`www.collegegrad.com/jobsearch/intro.shtml`

Author Brian Krueger's book, *College Grad Job Hunter,* though available in bookstores, is also available online. For free. The book is aimed at the college graduate, emphasizing techniques to use when you have book learning, but not much real-world experience. He also points out that job-hunting is an experience that you should start preparing for before it happens, and there is a lot of good advice for all job-hunters. I think that some of his guerilla tactics should be avoided, but this is a minor complaint; it's a great online resource.

Career Playbook

`www.careerplaybook.com/guide/tour_overview.asp`

If you don't mind the football analogy central to this site, this is a pretty good guide. It stresses the importance of having a plan for your job-hunt, and it backs it up with good advice.

JOB-HUNTING ARTICLES

The Web is now brimming with articles about job-hunting; as time passes, it's becoming more difficult to find the ones that burn brightest in a field that tends to generate more heat than light. The ones I have listed here are all good, for various reasons. Note that more links to articles about Internet research, contacts, resumes, and job boards are in the chapters that cover those topics.

The Dirty Dozen Online Job-Hunting Mistakes

`www.job-hunt.org/ jobsearchmistakes.shtml`

Good one, from one of the best Gateway job sites.

The Truth about Online Job Hunting

`www.careerjournal.com/jobhunting/ usingnet/20020417-needleman.html`

Though not extensive or earthshaking, this article is a good, basic primer on Internet job-hunting. More about attitudes than actions, the article will help to dispel a number of false assumptions and point you down the right road. You'll find many helpful articles on the *Wall Street Journal*'s website, so be sure you explore it thoroughly.

A Yellow Wood
`http://yw.english.ucsb.edu`

The site's subtitle is "Diverging Career Pathways for Humanities Ph.D.s," but these articles aren't just for Ph.D.s. Anyone majoring in the humanities (or liberal arts) and wondering what on earth to do after graduation may benefit. Under the heading of Travelogs, it's got an interesting series of articles by humanities majors about how they found their way into various industries (not predictable from their major). Paths links to job boards and job listings in nonacademic career paths, while Status Quo has articles on the current and future state of the job market for humanities graduates. The site is starting to show just a little age—there are some broken links—but it's still quite valuable.

Common Job Search Misconceptions
`www.wetfeet.com/asp/article.asp`
`?aid=105&atype=Interviewing`

A very good article, and if you browse the WetFeet site, you'll find many others that are just as good.

Forum: Ask the Hiring Manager
`www.collegegrad.com/forum/index.shtml`

Another good feature from CollegeGrad.com. The CollegeGrad site is aimed—this will strain my credibility, I know—at recent college graduates, who usually lack experience at the job-hunt game. The site has a lot to offer everyone, recent college graduate or not; this particular page is a series of questions answered by author Brian Kreuger, about different aspects of the job-hunt.

On the same site, check out the Ezine at `www.collegegrad`
`.com/ezine/index.shtml`, where you will find a list of
links to past articles.

Informational Interviewing
`http://danenet.wicip.org/jets/jet-9407-p.html`

This important technique is explained and discussed at this site.
While the site makes this technique a bit more complex than it
needs to be, it still provides a good overview.

Informational Interviewing Tutorial
`www.quintcareers.com/informational`
`_interviewing.html`

Another Quintessential Careers home run: one of the best and
most complete articles (actually, it is a series of articles) on the
subject available.

Monster's Virtual Interview
`http://interview.monster.com/`
`virtualinterview/campus`

This site, part of the Monster Network, has a "virtual interview"
exercise, which gives you the opportunity to practice a hiring interview. It offers you questions with multiple-choice answers and
tells you whether or not you chose the best answer. If you didn't,
it gives you a chance to try and choose a better answer the second
time around. Trouble is, while some of the questions are cute, in
the case of the more serious questions, I didn't think any of the
answers offered was the correct one to give! It needs "none of
the above" as an option. Oh well. Take it with a grain of salt, and
enjoy.

THE GATEWAY SITES AND MORE

This would be as good a place as any to reiterate that the Gateway
sites I mentioned in chapter 1 (and which I list again here) are excellent places for advice and information about job-hunting.
Also, the Supersites have many articles of value, though the sites
listed below will *usually* be better:

Job-Hunt
`www.job-hunt.org`

One of the best of the Gateway sites, run by Susan Joyce. A wealth of information on job-hunting, using the Internet effectively, and current articles about the world of work. Past issues of the Job-Hunt newsletter, the *Online Job Search Guide,* are also available at the site.

JobStar
`www.jobstar.org`

Lots of good information for the job-hunter; particularly good when looking for information on salaries and the Hidden Job Market.

The Riley Guide
`www.rileyguide.com`

With informative and timely articles, the Riley Guide is one of the best job-hunt sites on the Web.

Quintessential Careers
`www.quintcareers.com`

Many articles on job-hunting, resumes, testing, and career assessment. Note that you must use Internet Explorer for some parts of the site to work properly.

Career InfoNet Reading Room
`www.acinet.org/acinet/rr_Research.asp`

Part of Career InfoNet, which is itself part of the government's triumvirate of job-hunting websites. Many valuable articles here.

Careers.Org Career Library
`www.careers.org/06_cref.html`

From Careers.Org, a site with lots of information; particularly good for college students.

Job-Hunter's Bible
www.jobhuntersbible.com

> From the author of *What Color Is Your Parachute?* Here you will find many articles and resources for the job-hunter.

FOR FURTHER HELP: CAREER COUNSELING OFFICES

> If you still need more in the way of career counseling, you should take a look at all of the career offices on the Internet. There are essentially two kinds: career centers at colleges and universities and the various state government career offices. Though not traditionally renowned for their job-hunting acumen, many of the state employment development departments have improved mightily in the last few years. A few are surprisingly good.

College Career Centers
www.jobweb.com/Career_Development/
collegeres.htm

> From JobWeb, this is a list of career centers at colleges around the United States, as well as some in Canada, the United Kingdom, and Australia.

University Career Resources
www.careerresource.net/carserv

> This site has what appears to be a good list of career centers at various universities in the United States. I am disappointed that the list appears not to have been updated since September of 2000, but most of the links appear to be good despite this.

State Employment Offices
www.careers.org/topic/01_jobs_20.html

> You can access the Web pages of every U.S. state employment office from this alphabetical list (well ... *mostly* alphabetical; I always thought California came before Colorado).

ONE-ON-ONE CAREER COUNSELING

Your problem may be such that none of the resources I have listed, or that you have diligently searched for on your own, are able to help you. You may need the assistance of a professional. In this case, you are in luck:

Email a Career Counselor for Free
`www.jobhuntersbible.com/counseling/`
`request.shtml`

At the Job-Hunter's Bible site, we have a free service for people who have tried very hard to solve their job-hunt problems, but feel they are stuck. It is not the first place you should turn, but neither should you feel reticent about taking advantage of this unique resource. Go to this page for more information.

OFFLINE CAREER COUNSELING

In appendix C of *What Color Is Your Parachute?* you will find an extensive (and current) list of professional career counselors across the country and around the world. There's likely to be a career counselor near you, regardless of where you live. Some of the counselors listed are also willing to counsel through email or on the telephone.

The services of these professionals are not free, nor should you expect them to be. And you should not jump for a counselor as your first job-hunting move, substituting money for effort. But as with any licensed professional, be it a doctor, lawyer, or career counselor, there are times when you need to call for expert help.

EDUCATION

Maybe, after doing a lot of soul-searching, you have decided that you will never get the job or career you want without further education. Don't feel bad; there's a lot of that going around. Here are some places to start:

Yahoo! Education
`http://education.yahoo.com`

I happen to think that this is the most useful page that Yahoo! has, and that's saying quite a bit. From here, you can search for specific schools, look for schools that offer certain courses or degrees, even find out what schools have online classes, enabling you, in many cases, to get your degree over the Internet. Also a good place to check out K–12 schools for the kids, although I prefer the sites listed in chapter 2 under the heading of Work in Education. Anyway, a terrific site.

Academic Info
`www.academicinfo.net`

A great site for researching degree programs (online and offline), schools, test preparation . . . everything to do with education.

National Directory of Women's Education and Training Programs
`www.womenwork.org/resources/directory.htm`

Listed by state, this page gives you access to training and degree programs for women. Often, the accent is on displaced homemakers, working mothers, and women in transition.

Google University Search
`www.google.com/options/`
`universities.html`

This is a nice service, implemented strangely. From the extensive alphabetical list of universities, pick the one you want. That doesn't lead you to the school's Web page; it brings you to a database that Google has compiled, of what is on each university's Web server. You then need to enter a search term—"courses," "schedule," or the like—to get information. (I entered "*.*" out of habit, and got a browsable list of what was on the server.)

College Planning Resources
`www.quintcareers.com/college_planning.html`

A list of resources for people who are planning to attend college, adults who need to return to school, and so on.

Education Newsgroups
`www.careers.org/topic/03_lern_70.html`

A list of newsgroups dedicated to education.

Distance Learning
`www.careers.org/topic/03_lern_60.html`

A list of schools with online courses.

The Alternative Universe: A Guide $$
`http://query.nytimes.com/gst/abstract.html`
`?res=F50917FA3D5E0C768EDDAD0894DC404482`

This is an archived article on the *New York Times* website, by Julie Flaherty, listing colleges and universities that offer courses and degrees online. Well researched, with figures like total students, number of online students, and degrees and programs offered online. It will cost you $2.95 to read the article unless you already have an archive subscription.

CHAPTER FIVE

Job Sites

In previous editions of this book, I divided the websites where you can look at job listings and the sites where you can post your resume into two separate chapters. I did this not just because these are two different functions of the Internet but also because the sites listed in each chapter tended to be different places. But things have changed, as they will; it is now very rare to find a job site where you can do one thing, but not the other.

In the long run, this is better for both employer and job-hunter. It makes sense to have job postings and resume postings in the same place. You can still do everything you did when jobs and resumes were posted in different locations, and you still have the option of letting the computer do some of the work for you.

So, with that in mind, we can say that there are three things you can do at the job sites, also referred to as "job boards":

- You can look through the job listings in the site's database, using the on-site search engine that all such sites have. You type in keywords that you think will describe the jobs that you are interested in, and the search engine kicks back those job postings in its database that your keywords trigger.

- You can post your resume on the site. Employers can come to the site and look through the resumes that have been posted there, using the on-site search engine that all such sites have. Employers type in keywords that they think will describe the

151

people they are interested in finding, and the search engine kicks back those resumes in the site's database that the keywords trigger. Hopefully, one of those will be yours.

- Many job sites have the ability to match up resumes and job postings automatically; you could call them "matching engines." It's very much like typing in keywords to find a suitable job posting, but in this case, your resume itself takes the place of the search string. Most sites have the ability to do this continually, so that when a new job is posted to the site, even if it's days or weeks after you posted your resume, your posting and the job can still match up, and if they do, you will be notified by email.

What computers do quicker than people, if not better, is to say that *this* thing is the same as *that* thing, or that the two are different, and then take some action based on that sameness or difference. This action—the *conditional branch*—is the essence of *all* computer programming, and the technology is well suited to seeing if a resume matches a job posting. Or, more specifically, to see if the *keywords* in a resume match the keywords in a job posting. It's not the same thing.

Scientists have been working for half a century to get computers to understand what people mean, rather than what they say. They have yet to meet with real success; no surprise, when, after all these years, I'm not sure that I do it particularly well either. But you need to keep this principle in mind, if you are going to go on the job boards and enjoy any real success: you will have to learn to think, at least a little bit, in the very literal manner in which a computer thinks. When searching through job postings, you will have to think of the right keywords to bring up the sort of job you are interested in. The perfect job could be *right there,* just a mouse click away, but if you cannot enter the proper keywords for the job site's matching engine to bring it to your attention, the job might as well be on Mars.

You will quickly see what this means when you write your resume. It must be written with the specific goal of responding to any keywords that an employer might enter, as he looks for potential employees. Additionally, if you are going to submit your resume to the site's matching software, your resume must be written so that it will also trigger that software; and yet, it must still be readable. This is an art.

Lucky for you, I'm not the only person to have thought about this, and there are many websites that will tell you how to write your resume for the Internet age. In fact, there is an embarrassment of riches when it comes to Internet resume resources. But let me digress for a moment.

Many of the sites one finds on the Internet are a mix of commercial offers and free resources. You should never feel bad about taking advantage of these free resources, even when you have no intention of ever purchasing something at the site. Generally, the sites' owners put up the free resources to attract people to the site; they know that a certain percentage will become paying customers. This is a financial model used throughout the Web.

However, you'll see that when you start visiting resume sites, the commercial temperature rises considerably. As you go on these sites to avail yourself of the resources to be found there, you will have to wade through more than the usual number of offers for books, audiotapes, or whatever. And of course, the materials offered for sale contain the two (or maybe it's seven; I forget) secrets that *you absolutely must know* in order to achieve job-hunting success. You may be doomed to failure if you don't order today!

My advice to you is to live without these secrets if you are going to have to pay for them. There is *so* much free info about resumes on the Web, there's a chance you'll stumble on those five (or was it eight?) secrets to success anyway. If you spend the requisite time and effort at this on your own, and eventually come to believe you need more assistance, then you can always purchase later.

That said, let's look at:

RESUMES AND COVER LETTERS

JobStar Central
www.jobstar.org/tools/resume/index.cfm

If I were interested in putting an electronic resume on the Internet, and if I could visit only one site for guidance and help, JobStar would be it, no question. This site, the creation of Mary-Ellen

Mort, features excellent information (and links to more of same) about writing resumes for Net consumption. There are links to sample resumes, and the subject of cover letters is also, uh, covered.

CareerJournal Resumes
`www.careerjournal.com/jobhunting/resumes`

From the masters of business at the *Wall Street Journal*'s Career-Journal, here's a series of articles pertaining to resumes. Most are short and to the point; you will need to read a number of them to get the big picture, but the picture is there.

ProvenResumes.com
`www.provenresumes.com/toc.html`

From Regina Pontow's *Proven Resumes* site, some very helpful articles about resume writing.

Career Development eManual:
Resumes and Cover Letters
`www.cdm.uwaterloo.ca/step4_2.asp`

From the Career Center at the University of Waterloo in Ontario, Canada, comes this section on resumes and cover letters. Leans a bit toward the graduating college student—it *is* a school, after all—but excellent all the same.

How to Write a Resume Masterpiece
`www.rockportinstitute.com/resumes.html`

An article from the Rockport website. I particularly like the page with "power words" that you can incorporate.

Creative Job Search Online Guide: Resumes
`www.deed.state.mn.us/cjs/resume.htm`

In the job-search manual from Minnesota's Department of Employment and Economic Development, there is a good set of guidelines for resume writing, with excellent sample resumes.

200 Letters for Job-Hunters
`www.careerlab.com/letters/default.htm`

Turning from resumes to cover letters, here's the best collection of them on the Internet. William S. Frank has put his entire book, *200 Letters for Job-Hunters*, online for free. So now, if you want to write something during your job-hunt, but just don't know how to write it, come to this site. There are cover letters galore, cold-call letters, thank-you letters (nineteen of them), letters helping you to leave a job gracefully, how to negotiate a pay raise, and so on.

Cover Letters
`www.career.vt.edu/JOBSEARC/coversamples.htm`

From the Career Services office at Virginia Tech comes this excellent article on cover letters, with samples of same, including email versions.

Resume Resources for Job-Seekers
`www.quintcareers.com/resres.html`

From the Quintessential Careers site, a (long) list of (good) resume articles.

Gary Will's Worksearch
`www.garywill.com/worksearch`

Canadian author and job expert Gary Will has done a marvelous job writing cogent and insightful articles.

Tips on Resume Writing
`www.montana.edu/~wwwcp/tips.html`

This is not an article in itself, but a page of links to other sources, most of which are quite good.

15 Tips for Writing Winning Resumes
`www.questcareer.com/tips.htm`

Okay, so it was fifteen. Nice little article.

WetFeet Resumes
`www.wetfeet.com/advice/resumes.asp`

On the bottom half of this Web page is a list of resume articles. Each examines one facet of writing a resume and associated activities; most are very helpful.

For-Fee Resume Services $$
`http://dir.yahoo.com/Business_and_Economy/`
`Shopping_and_Services/Employment/`
`Resume_Services`

`http://directory.google.com/Top/Business/`
`Employment/Resumes_and_Portfolios`

Reduced to tears at the thought of having to write your own cover letter and resume (electronic or otherwise), even with all these aids online? If you are determined to go this route, and the services offered on the websites I have listed don't grab you, then there's a few hundred more for-fee resume and cover letter services in these two directories.

How do you evaluate who's good and who's not? Ask to see samples of resumes that actually resulted in jobs for their clients. Ask to talk to the client to confirm that this is so. Some resume writers will balk at this request; good ones won't.

RESUME TIPS

Some of the advice you'll get in these articles will be contradictory. When that happens, go with what your mind tells you makes the most sense. Also, here are a few other tips:

- You should have two versions of your resume: one that you will use in the body of an email and a nicer, more professional version that you will use for all other situations. Be sure to read the section in chapter 3 on resumes and email.

- Experts differ on whether you should return to the job boards to "refresh" your resume; some career writers advise doing this every few days so that employers won't view yours as being "old" or out-of-date. I don't advise doing this more often than every two weeks or so; if you do, be sure to remove the old one. Also, if you are hired somewhere, do everyone a favor and remove your resume from the boards where you posted it.

- Don't apply to the same employer for more than one position, tweaking your resume each time to more closely match each job listing. This can only lead to problems.

- When posting your resume online, there is nothing wrong with having a "keywords" line at the bottom of the page, where you list words, appropriate to your experience and skills, that are designed solely to snag the site's search engine when an employer is doing a resume search. Just write the word *Keywords*, followed by a colon and the appropriate terms separated by commas. Preferably, these keywords should not take up more than a single line, two at the most. Remember, this is *only* for resumes posted online!

PORTFOLIOS

An alternative to the written resume is a pictorial resume, often called a "portfolio." It's not just pretty pictures; it offers proof that you have the skills you claim to have. Certain professions are known for using a portfolio (artists, models, craftsmen, and so on). But in the '80s and '90s, under the influence of books by career experts Eugene Williams, Martin Kimeldorf, and others, the idea has been expanded to include many other types of work.

Portfolio Library
`http://amby.com/kimeldorf/portfolio`

Here Martin Kimeldorf describes in great detail his view of what a portfolio can be—the why, the wherefore, and the how-to. His form is not by any means the only way to go—it's long, and directed at educational situations—but it may stimulate your own creativity.

AFTER THE RESUME

Beyond resumes, the next step is the job boards themselves. Before we dive in there, read up a little about how to approach the boards:

Beyond Resume Posting
`www.jobsinthemoney.com/html/docid/resume`
`_posting.html`

Okay, you've posted your resume, now what do you do? This will tell you.

Using Web Job Sites
`www.job-hunt.org/jobsearchusing.shtml`

Keeping Track of Your Job Search
`www.job-hunt.org/jobsearchtracking.shtml`

The Dirty Dozen Online Job Search Mistakes
`www.job-hunt.org/jobsearchmistakes.shtml`

A triumvirate of excellent articles from Susan Joyce at Job-Hunt.

Before you assume that you'll get a job through the Internet, remember that posting a job opening on a job site almost always costs the employer money. And if an employer can hire someone more cheaply or easily, he or she will take another route. As a result, the job postings that you will find on these sites tend to be openings that are just a little harder to fill than otherwise, from the employer's perspective. You might reasonably conclude, then, that the job postings on these sites will require higher levels of experience and education than you have, or they may be slightly less desirable than jobs found elsewhere, else they would not be listed here.

But exceptions are legion, and people *do* find work through these sites. There is no reason why you can't be one of them, is there? Of course not! So that just leaves one question: which job boards are best?

Unfortunately, there's no single site where all the jobs in the world are listed. In fact, there are *thousands* of different job sites and many different databases of job listings. Even so, it makes sense to go where the *most* job postings and resumes are. After all, if you put your resume where there are, say, a hundred jobs available, you would not be as likely to find that perfect job as if you went to a site where there are *thousands*. And so, it is inevitable that you would look at the Supersites.

The Supersites—Monster, CareerBuilder, HotJobs, and America's Job Bank—have, traditionally at least, worked best for those in the IT field; worked next best for those with executive, managerial, or technical backgrounds; and worked hardly at all for low-tech and manufacturing jobs. As more people have come to the Net to conduct their job-hunts, the Supersites' effectiveness has probably improved, although there is still no real data to say how much. The Supersites themselves have released no figures on their own effectiveness that I have ever seen.

But what you want to know is: right now, are they worth trying? The simple answer is okay, sure, why not? Which is not the same as an emphatic yes. I don't think you should *only* use the Supersites; you should explore the specialized and niche sites as well. And there are a few things to remember when using job boards, and the Supersites, in particular:

- For the most part, the "extras" that they have for helping job-hunters—articles, quizzes, sample resumes and cover letters, and so on—are done better at the Gateway job sites like Job-Hunt, JobStar, and the Riley Guide.

- With notable exceptions (America's Job Bank would be one), most job boards are commercial ventures. When they offer services for money, check around to make sure that the same services and quality (if not better) can't be found elsewhere for free.

- Many of the job listings on Monster, CareerBuilder, and America's Job Bank are not for actual jobs; they are really just advertisements, placed by agencies and recruiters. If you end up getting a job through one of them, there are likely to be fees involved, and they may have to be paid by you. These ads-disguised-as-jobs happen on many job boards; obviously, you should try to avoid them. They are generally easy to spot: when you look at the details of a job, it will mention that it is a "third-party listing." These ads help to make the advertised number of job listings in the sites' databases meaningless.

- When you put your resume up on a job board, you generally lose control over what happens to it after that. Read the privacy policy very carefully before you post. Some sites have received complaints in the past about how their customers' data was used. If you don't like the terms of the site's agreement, don't post.

- Particularly with the Supersites, job listings on one job board are not generally on any of the others. That means that if you are going to use one, you should probably use more than one if you want the best chance of finding a job—remember, this is a numbers game. The extra time is minimal and may make the difference for you.

Yahoo! HotJobs
`http://hotjobs.yahoo.com`

This is not the largest of the Supersites by far, but the quality of the listings in its jobs database tends to be better than the others, largely because it does not accept "job listings" (ads) from agencies and recruiters.

As with the other Supersites, employers are charged to list their job openings or to search resumes, while services are free to the job-hunter once you register. (HotJobs doesn't seem to have any mechanism for culling out old accounts and user names, so you might have to go through the registration page a few times until you find a user name that has never been used at one time or another.) In my brief sampling of jobs in the database, I found more than a thousand postings each for nurses and CPAs (when returning results, the HotJobs search engine is not specific about numbers more than a thousand), thirty-two electronics techs, no research biologists, and ninety cabinetmakers.

Notably, HotJobs brings Yahoo!'s resources and experience to the table in the community and networking arena. For example, if you click on the Communities link, you will see a list of about thirty-five professions—legal, telecommunications, government, health care, accounting and finance, the list goes on—where you can join in discussions with people seeking work in these various

fields. As with all such chat facilities, you do need to choose what you read carefully; there is a lot of complaining here, but that aside, there is still information to be had and contacts to be made.

I have made Hotjobs a Parachute Pick in this category, not because it has the largest database of job listings but because it doesn't accept agency and recruiter listings, so its database contains only real jobs. This is not to say that you shouldn't try the others as well, but if you are going to use the Supersites, I would recommend you start here first.

Monster
www.monster.com

Arguably the best known of all the job-hunting sites on the Internet, Monster has many thousands of job listings, from all over the United States. It has the best name recognition of all of the boards, and why not? It advertises during the Super Bowl.

Besides letting you search its listings by keyword, geographic area, and industry, Monster also has a Job Search Agent, which is a software program that will examine new listings as they are created and will email you the ones that match your criteria. In a few test searches, without regard to location, I found more than 5,000 listings for registered nurses, 2,600 positions for electronic technicians, more than 1,200 listings for truck drivers (though most were just ads from truck-driving schools), and 4 positions for cabinetmakers. There were 70 nationwide positions for research biologists and more than 5,000 positions for CPAs.

Monster's basic services are free to the job-hunter, although you must register; it is funded by employers' job listings and by online advertisers (with some pop-up ads).

America's Job Bank
www.ajb.dni.us

If you want proof that the government occasionally does something right, you might start here. Sponsored by the Department of Labor and the employment development departments of the fifty states, it is free to both employers and job-hunters. Last I visited, it claimed more than 1.25 million job listings in the database and almost 700,000 resumes.

CHAPTER FIVE

Since a large part of the job listings comes from state EDDs, this is not a bad place to go if you are looking for jobs in state or local government, school districts, state-run secondary education, public utilities, and so forth. Not all of the jobs listed here are perfect, but there *are* a lot of them. In my little survey, I found almost 7,000 listings for CPAs, 415 for cabinetmakers, more than 30,000 for registered nurses, 1,700 for electronics technicians, and 250 for research biologists. However, I should mention that the matching engine software used by this site cuts an extremely wide swath: for example, the search for research biologist kicked back listings for archaeologist and senior city planner, among others. You are allowed to sort the job listings by relevance to your search keywords, but there is still a lot of chaff to be culled out. As with the other Supersites, you can look for jobs based on various criteria, and there is an automatic Search Scout that will email you as possible job listings come in that match your criteria.

The site is well laid out and thought out and is slow to point you to other resources that are fee based.

CareerBuilder
www.careerbuilder.com

CareerBuilder is jointly owned by the Tribune Company, Gannett, and Knight-Ridder—newspaper companies all. This means that it not only accepts paid postings from employers but its listings include the want ads from about two hundred newspapers across the country. As a result, the database is huge, and because of the newspaper origin of many of the postings, you will find more lower-tech and traditionally blue-collar jobs listed here. In my unscientific sampling, I found positions for 25 cabinetmakers, 3,300 truck drivers (again, most were ads), close to 22,000 registered nurses (many from agencies), 980 electronic techs, more than 5,000 CPAs, and 87 research biologists.

Registering with the site allows you to search its database by keyword, field, and location; it offers newsletters and other services. Because of the site's newspaper background, it also partners with websites that offer apartment rentals, autos for sale, and networking (through Tribe.net) across the country. You can sign up to receive emailed information about career fairs in your area, as well as the site's *Cool Jobs* newsletter, which highlights certain jobs and companies that use CareerBuilder for hiring.

This site is more commercially oriented than the other Super-sites, and there are certainly more pop-up ads. I was struck by the site's Resources page; most links on the page lead to a fee-based offer rather than to the more typical free Internet resource.

REGIONAL JOB SITES

RegionalHelpWanted.com
`http://regionalhelpwanted.com/corporate/our_sites_usa.cfm`

I would wager that you have never heard of Regional Help Wanted. But I'd bet you *have* heard of Bay Area Help Wanted dot com, or Help Wanted Phoenix dot com, or Central Illinois Help Wanted dot com, and so on—currently 283 of them in the United States and Canada. Using the standard fee-to-employer, free-to-job-hunter model, the site's innovative radio ad campaign has helped to establish Regional Help Wanted across the country in record time.

Job-hunters can click on the map at the page listed above, or go to the alphabetical city listing at `http://regionalhelp wanted.com/corporate/our_sites.cfm` and find the nearest one (the map will clearly indicate areas without a local board). Once there, you will find a better-than-average job board, with very complete job descriptions (there's effectively no limit on the number of words employers can use to describe a job listing). The ratio of jobs available to job-seekers registered varies widely and wildly from one board to another in the system; you should check and see what's available in your area.

craigslist
`www.craigslist.org`

Started in San Francisco, craigslist has spread to more than fifty cities around the United States and the world. Though more of a community bulletin board than your typical job board, craigslist is a site you ignore at your peril when job-hunting. Why? Because there are *tons* of jobs here. As well as the typical range of jobs, there are others here that may interest you, particularly if you are looking for a job with a smaller business, if your work is more creative than most, or if you want to tap into areas of employment that might be somewhat out of the mainstream. Additionally, if you are starving and need some quick hourly or by-the-job work, the "gigs" section can be a life-saver—or an apartment-saver, or a car-payment maker.

There are craigslist sites for (deep breath) Albuquerque, Anchorage, Atlanta, Austin, Baltimore, Boise, Boston, Buffalo, Charlotte, Chicago, Cincinnati, Cleveland, Columbus, Dallas, Denver, Detroit, Fresno, Hartford, Honolulu, Houston, Indianapolis, Kansas City, Las Vegas, Los Angeles, Memphis, Miami, Milwaukee, Minneapolis, Nashville, New Orleans, New York, Norfolk, Orlando, Philadelphia, Phoenix, Pittsburgh, Portland, Providence, Raleigh, Sacramento, Salt Lake City, San Diego, San Francisco, Santa Barbara, Seattle, St. Louis, Tampa Bay, Washington, D.C., Montreal, Toronto, and Vancouver. By the time you read this, there should be sites for Albany, Jacksonville, Louisville, Oklahoma City, Omaha, Richmond, San Antonio, Tucson, Tulsa, and Ottawa.

Overseas, you'll find craigslist in Dublin, Edinburgh, London, Manchester, Melbourne, and Sydney, with sites soon in Adelaide, Amsterdam, Auckland, Bangalore, Barcelona, Birmingham, Brisbane, Hong Kong, Manila, Mexico City, Paris, and Tokyo.

JobDig
www.jobdig.com

This is the website of a popular (and free) job newspaper of the same name, which publishes weekly regional issues for cities in Minnesota, Iowa, Nebraska, and the Dakotas. Currently headquartered in Minneapolis, they are growing rapidly into other markets. The website lists many jobs for the covered areas—you can search for a job by location, job type, or employer, and the on-site employer directory is a neat feature. You can also view the various regional issues of the paper online, which contain helpful articles by well-known experts in the work and job-hunting fields, as well as the published job listings and employer ads. Very well done.

Jobs in Maine
`http://jobsinme.com/home/home.aspx`

Jobs in New Hampshire
`http://jobsinnh.com/home/home.aspx`

Jobs in Rhode Island
`http://jobsinri.com/home/home.aspx`

Jobs in Massachusetts
`http://jobsinma.com/home/home.aspx`

Jobs in Vermont
`http://jobsinvt.com/home/home.aspx`

If you live in New England, you have an extra resource available in the form of these award-winning job sites. Originally started as Jobs in Maine, the site expanded to include the five current states. If you don't live in one of these five, you might try `http://jobsintheus.com/jobsintheus/default.asp` to see if they have one now for where you live.

THE NETWORKED SITES

At the risk of sounding repetitious, there are many thousands of job-hunting sites on the Web (as of 2004, the accepted figure in the industry is forty thousand, but how accurate that figure is, or where it came from, I have no idea). Although few of the databases for these many job boards are identical, there *are* many that are similar.

Here's why: most websites that want to offer job-hunting services to their clientele can't, because there's no good way to begin.

Without a database of resumes and job listings to start with, they can't attract employers and job-hunters to their site to post their resumes and job listings. They need something to jump-start the process before they can attract enough employers and job-hunters to their sites to build up their databases to a useful level.

A number of companies have leaped in to offer just such a jump-start package to these sites: kind of a "job board in a box"; just add website, job-hunters, and employers. I am aware of four major companies that appear to offer this core database and search software package: FlipDog, CareerBuilder, BestJobsUSA, and 4Jobs. It's likely there are others as well, but those are the four I've noticed. A niche site using one of these services will, naturally, add new listings and resumes from and for its special clientele, which will tend to make its database somewhat unique to its site, but many listings are shared among sites as well.

I have listed a variety of job boards in this chapter, but I have made no effort to try to list even all of the good ones; there are just too many. If you click around to a number of them, you will start seeing the similarities and differences that identify these four primary sites. Along with the sites I have listed, look at the directories of job boards; there could easily be a special job board for your field with job listings that might only be found there. But use your sense: you don't have the time to sign up at a hundred different job sites, and it's unlikely that doing so would substantially raise your employment prospects.

FlipDog.com
`http://flipdog.monster.com`

FlipDog is now owned by Monster, and has the look and feel of that popular site, if not the same database of jobs and resumes.

4Jobs.com
`www.4jobs.com`

It isn't the best; it's certainly not the worst. 4Jobs is typical of many job sites on the Web, and for very good reason: it *is* many job sites on the Web. 4Jobs serves as the software and core database for hundreds—*hundreds*—of Internet job boards. You should visit it just because its network is so extensive.

JobBank USA
`www.jobbankusa.com/search.html`

All in all, a slightly better-than-average job board. There are job-hunting resources and articles at the site, as well as the standard database of job postings; most are recently dated. What the site lists as a meta-search function is mostly a hosting function for other websites that have job listings, such as newspaper and niche boards. As is typical with this software, the search agent cuts a pretty wide swath; a search for "registered nurse" positions yielded, among other things, a posting for a patent attorney. Hmmm.

Anyway, the site is not bug free, but it does have a kind of personality, and I think that the total is somehow more than just the sum of its parts.

COLLEGE AND GRADUATE SITES

CollegeGrad.com
`www.collegegrad.com`

I *love* this site. There is no better one available on the Internet for the college student or recent graduate. Excellent resources, good job database, with all the features such a site should have. Well done, Brian Krueger.

CollegeJournal
`www.collegejournal.com`

Another of the *Wall Street Journal*'s many arms, this one is as professional as the others. Good database, better than average resources.

AfterCollege
`www.aftercollege.com`

Focuses on internships and entry-level and summer jobs.

CollegeRecruiter.com
`www.collegerecruiter.com`

Entry-level and internships.

NICHE, TRADE, SPECIALTY

There are about a bazillion niche job boards—I should know, it feels like I've been to every one of them. Here is what amounts to only a sampling of what is available for various trades, industries, and professions. I have tried *not* to list the sites that are part of the major job-site networks, preferring instead to find job boards that were independently operated and well thought of in their particular industry; I have not always been successful.

Note that I have not attempted to be complete or fair. As the mother goose said to her gosling while pointing out an ostrich egg, I just want you to see the possibilities. If these aren't enough, and you want to find more job boards in your area of expertise or interest, go to a search engine and type in "[some profession] jobs," of course substituting your area of interest for "some profession." A list will come up of sites for you to try.

FindLaw
`http://careers.findlaw.com`

The best of the legal job sites, in my opinion. A good database with law jobs of every description, from judge through summer associate, office manager, law librarian, even temps, all searchable by location and area of specialty. Outplacement resources, suggestions for nonmainstream legal positions . . . there's even a section where us non-lawyers can find an attorney nearby, who practices in the required specialty. Well done.

The Law Employment Center
`www.lawjobs.com`

In addition to its database of legal jobs for attorneys, paralegals, legal secretaries, and the like, the site also includes temp positions, employment trends, and other useful info for the job-seeker. As with most legal job sites, a quick look through its employer directory reveals that most jobs listed are through legal recruiting firms. What is true in many fields seems true in the legal profession as well: most jobs are found through networking.

Legal Career Center Network
`www.thelccn.com`

Not accessible to the average person (or book writer), this is a service that is offered through various professional organizations. Check with your local bar, paralegal, or legal assistant association to see if it offers access to members.

EmplawyerNet $$
`www.emplawyernet.com`

Unlike most job sites, EmplawyerNet charges the job-hunter and is free to the employer. EmplawyerNet.com charges $125 a year to access its database of (currently 3,779) legal jobs (down from 4,858 two years ago).

On the plus side, the site does have a free directory of legal recruiters and employers around the country, grouped by city and state. Since so many law jobs are through recruiters anyway, you might skip the fee and go straight to the recruiter list, using the site as a research resource only.

TrueCareers
`www.truecareers.com`

Though TrueCareers bills itself as a job board for "degreed professionals," and its database does indeed include listings for civil engineer, Java developer, senior tax associate, architect, airport engineer, and so forth, there were also listings (and ads mixed with listings, of course) for delivery drivers and salesmen. Really smart ones, I guess.

But most of the positions are for what I think of as high trades—engineering, accounting, project management—like that. Pop-up ads are incessant and very persistent.

BioSpace
`www.biospace.com/career_main.cfm`

The Career Center page of this biotechnology website, with the standard industry-oriented job and resume databases, is searchable by location, salary, company, and specialty. An interesting little tool is the Job Assessor, where you rate the different aspects of two possible jobs, side by side, and then come up with a final score to indicate the more desirable.

StyleCareers
`www.stylecareers.com`

A job board for people in the fashion industry: apparel, footwear, home fashion, beauty, textiles. Actual positions run the fullest possible range: hair stylist to photographer to purchasing agent to color specialist to makeup artist . . .

AllRetailJobs.com
`www.allretailjobs.com`

The name kind of says it all, doesn't it?

Creative Hotlist
`http://creativehotlist.com/`
`index.asp`

A job board for people in the creative arts, such as photographers, graphic artists, art directors, artists of every stripe, and so on. When you register, you receive a URL on the site that points prospective employers straight to your profile, with your personal data and links to any examples of your work that you've posted. An interesting feature is that you can post portfolios as well as resumes (the cost is $35 for six months; everything else on the site is free). A neat site.

Jobs for PhDs
`http://jobs.phds.org/jobs`

As job boards go, this one is pretty quirky; I guess it reflects the personality of a lot of those Ph.D. types (maybe I should have listed it under "Diversity"?) The chances of the average reader of this book finding a job here are almost nil. I like it a lot.

MedHunters
`www.medhunters.com`

Health-care jobs—more than eleven thousand at last count—are listed here; a superior site. One of the nice touches is that it groups jobs so that you can browse by lifestyle, such as, sun, mountains, coastal, exotic, major sports nearby, rural and small town . . . neat, huh?

Jobscience
`www.jobscience.com`

Another good health-care niche board.

HealthCareersUSA.com
`www.healthcareersusa.com`

Part of the BestJobsUSA network, this site specializes in, obviously, jobs in the health industry. I haven't listed too many of the BestJobsUSA sites; I find the software buggy and aspects of the database are incomplete. But . . . there are a number of sites in their net, so it might be worth checking.

The Blue Line
`www.theblueline.com`

Law enforcement, fire, and civilian law (dispatcher, etc.) positions.

ComputerJobs.com
`www.computerjobs.com/homepage.aspx`

Tech jobs of all descriptions are available through this site. A number of excellent features are here; these include listing the number of jobs available in various cities, listing jobs by various specialties and skills, and the ability to click on a city to see the jobs available in that city, sorted by specialty. My latest visit showed almost ten thousand job listings, with a quarter of those being less than a week old; an excellent currency rate for an Internet job board and what at least *appears* to be proof that these jobs are getting filled.

Computerwork.com
`http://computerwork.com`

Another good job site for the IT professional. Decent-size database, all of the features of the better job boards, plus a few extra features, including a special link for reporting outdated jobs in the database—surprisingly rare.

techies.com
`www.techies.com`

Another good job board for IT people. Linked with different local boards like bayareatechies.com and chicagotechies.com, you'll find plenty of listings for technical jobs.

Construction Jobs
`http://construction.careercast.com`

A job board for the construction, building, and design industries. Nice implementation; jobs tend toward the higher end, as in management, architecture, and so on, but there are also many handyman and custodial positions. I am reminded here of how literal the software on the job boards can be: a search on "heavy equipment" brings up everything from "registered nurse" to "temporary warehouse person." Because I didn't put the terms in quotes, to force processing them together as a phrase, the site kicked back a huge range of jobs. Almost every job description here has the word *equipment* in it!

Mechanical, Electrical, Plumbing at Work
`www.mepatwork.com`

MEP at Work is a job board for those seeking jobs in the trades, such as HVAC, plumbing, electrical, and so on. The database is a

shared one and it contains an unfortunately low incidence of jobs in the trades, but perhaps that will improve with time.

Dice

www.dice.com

Long a popular board for people in the tech industries, as well as author of various IT industry and salary reports, Dice has recently expanded its database to include jobs in biotech, aerospace, and engineering. During my last visit, it claimed to have more than fifty thousand current jobs listings; that's a lot of jobs. Dice's database serves as the database for a number of other tech job sites.

EmploymentGuide.com

www.employmentguide.com

Kind of a job board for everyman. Beauticians, carpet cleaners, handymen, delivery drivers, like that. It gives links to other, more specialized, boards for certain niche areas, like health care. Annoyingly, but not unusually, some ads are mixed in with the job listings.

Similar to the classifieds in the newspaper, sometimes you just need to see what jobs are available in your area before you even know what job titles you should search for; that's why I like it when job boards allow you to browse through all of the available jobs in your area. EmploymentGuide lets you do just that, with the names of employers included, a nice feature.

AutoJobs.com
`www.autojobs.com`

A job board for those in the automobile industry. Most of the jobs listed are in support industries, such as dealerships and repair facilities, but there are also jobs grouped under manufacturers, management, and aftermarket manufacturing, as well as under sales, sales management, body shop, technician, service, and office personnel.

HCareers
`www.hcareers.com`

Many companies have turned to the Internet for hiring now, and the service industry is certainly no different. Wal-Mart. Taco Bell. Circuit City. Marriott. Blockbuster. Hilton. Red Lobster. At the HCareers site (actually, a group of three sites), you'll find hospitality, restaurant, and retail jobs—more than forty thousand of them. You can search by management or nonmanagement, type of business, area, and so forth. There are links to overseas service jobs as well. An *excellent* site.

SHRM Jobs
`http://shrm.org/jobs`

From the Society for Human Resource Management, this job board is for people in the human resources field: payroll, HR managers, benefits analysts, recruiters, HR personnel, and so on. A nice feature is the Between Gigs forum and bulletin board, where you can talk and share job leads with others.

jobsinthemoney.com

`www.jobsinthemoney.com`

Loan officer, accountant, finance manager, tax analyst. If you are looking for a job in the finance industry, this is a good place to start.

Medzilla

`http://medzilla.com`

A job board for pharmaceutical, biotech, science, and health-care jobs. This one is a website with character—I like the design. You can search the job listings or browse the employer database to see what's available.

ServeNet

`www.servenet.org/cont/control_cont_item`
`_view.cfm?contentTypeId=4&hlpcat=8&tip=on`

From the ServeNet site, this is a list of current job openings with nonprofit or social-conscience organizations.

Teachers Support Network
`www.teacherssupportnetwork.com`

A job-hunting site for teachers. Services are free, though you must register. I list this as part of my "no teacher left behind" philosophy.

National Teacher Recruitment Clearinghouse
`www.recruitingteachers.org/channels/`
`clearinghouse/index.asp`

Good job site for teachers.

Chronicle Careers—Careers in Higher Education

`http://chronicle.com/jobs`

From the *Chronicle of Higher Education* comes this really excellent job site. At my last visit, there were jobs in its database from almost 1,100 institutions of higher learning, with openings all across the spectrum, from university president to tenured posts to lab assistant to groundskeeper. Resources include advice on how to turn your CV into a resume, salary calculators, Web links related to academic careers, and a forum for discussing these and other subjects. Top-notch.

Jobs in Education
`www.jobsineducation.com/new_pages/Job`
`percent20Seekers/job_seekers_info.htm`

A Canadian job site for K–12 institutions, listing academic, classified, business, and administration positions. On-site resources for finding out about certification requirements, salaries, and regional associations.

Jobs for Librarians
`www.lisjobs.com`

A job site for librarian and information professionals. Job listings are current, browsable, and searchable. There is also salary information for librarians, links to industry articles, and job-hunting advice. An email newsletter is available, and there are even links to overseas jobs in the profession. Good site.

EntertainmentCareers.Net
`www.entertainmentcareers.net`

A job board for those in film, television, and live theater, listing a huge range of jobs in broadcasting, television news (if you ever doubted that TV news was primarily entertainment, look where they advertise their job openings), production, film studios, theaters, and so on.

Idealist
`www.idealist.org/career.html`

Jobs and internships in public service and nonprofits.

Telecommuting Jobs
`www.tjobs.com`

Jobs that involve telecommuting or work-at-home.

Technical Writers Jobs
`http://tc.eserver.org/dir/Careers/`
`Job-Listings`

Not a job board itself, but a page of websites catering to jobs for technical writers and those in the professional, scientific, and technical communications fields.

DIVERSITY, WOMEN, DISABLED

LatPro
www.latpro.com

The best of the diversity boards, with excellent resources and an extremely large database. LatPro's high visibility attracts a lot of employers, which attracts many job-hunters, which attracts a lot of employers, which . . .

HireDiversity.com
www.hirediversity.com

Another excellent site. Good database, with articles and resources for African Americans, Asian Americans, Hispanics, disabled people, gays and lesbians, mature workers, veterans, and women.

WomensJobSearch.net
www.womensjobsearch.net

A job board specifically for women, obviously; the database looks similar to that of other job boards I have seen, and I doubt that the employers in the database were advertising *only* for women; that would be worrisome. More like the site is woman-friendly, with articles aimed at helping the working woman and mother.

Career Women
www.careerwomen.com

One of the leading women's boards.

disABLED person/recruitABILITY
www.disabledperson.com/RecruitABILITY/js.htm

disABLED person/recruitABILITY is a resume- and job-posting service, targeted toward the disabled and employers who are sensitive to their needs. The service is free to both job-hunter and employer.

WORKink
www.workink.com

A Canadian site designed for job-hunters with disabilities. There are job- and resume-posting services and other resources. It has an extensive—and very current—listing of jobs for the disabled on the site. Access is, of course, free.

GOVERNMENT JOBS

Federal Jobs Digest
www.jobsfed.com

You can browse this site's job listings by state and county or look through its occupational groupings. Search categories include salary, location, and job grouping.

USAJobs
www.usajobs.opm.gov

This is one of the U.S. government's official sites for jobs and employment information. It is absolutely current; and at my writing, contains almost seventeen thousand jobs. But this is by no means *all* of the jobs available with the federal government; many agencies use their own hiring resources, and you won't always find such jobs listed here.

FedWorld Federal Jobs Search
www.fedworld.gov/jobs/jobsearch.html

Another federal jobs site, with a pretty similar database to USAJobs, but possibly better search tools here.

CONTRACT AND TEMPORARY

Net Temps
www.nettemps.com

The site is excellent. Thousands of temp, contract, and permanent jobs; excellent articles and resources for the job-hunter; good links to other resources. Most of the jobs were current, and appeared legitimate (often, recruiters put in bogus jobs to try to sign up the desperate). If temp work is what you want (or need, for now), give this site a try.

JobSeek
www.staffingtoday.net/jobseek/index.html

Best way to find a temp agency on the Internet. Indicate your area, the kind of work you want, and it kicks back a list—sometimes a very *extensive* list—of temp agencies near you.

SummerJobs.com Location Search
www.summerjobs.com/jobSeekers/index.html

ResortJobs.com
www.resortjobs.com

InternJobs.com
www.internjobs.com

OverseasJobs.com
www.overseasjobs.com

These four sites are part of a network of job sites for "students, recent graduates, expatriates, and adventure seekers." Job openings around the world, primarily aimed at young people and the service industry. As is typical, the search agent cuts a broad swath, but the sites are good, nonetheless; great links pages, too.

Cool Works
`www.coolworks.com`

Links to thousands of jobs in national parks, resorts, cruises, camps, ski resorts, as well as ranch jobs and volunteering.

SnagAJob
`www.snagajob.com`

Part-time, restaurant, hourly, summer jobs . . . listings, resources, guidance, advice. Youth oriented, but not exclusively.

leisurejobs
`www.leisurejobs.com`

Not jobs where you lie around reading all day, but jobs at resorts and vacation spots. There are links to sister sites for the United Kingdom, Australia, and New Zealand.

Backdoorjobs.com
`www.backdoorjobs.com`

Summer situations and temporary, outdoor, and overseas jobs are listed. This is the website for *The Back Door Guide to Short-Term Job Adventures.*

ContractJobHunter $$
`www.cjhunter.com`

A job board for contract and consulting work; access will cost you a minimum of $25 per year, though you can search the employer database for free.

EXECUTIVE

6FigureJobs
`www.6figurejobs.com`

The premiere site for executive positions, top rated by everyone who does that sort of thing. Maybe a tad more commercial than the average job board.

ExecSearches.com

`www.execsearches.com/exec/default.asp`

A job board for executive and senior level positions with "non-profits, public sector, and socially responsible businesses." The Registry is its service that emails you with matching job postings.

CareerJournal

`www.careerjournal.com`

Mentioned often in this book as an excellent resource site, the *Wall Street Journal*'s careers website also has a job and resume database. Positions tend to be management and upper level, as you would expect.

Construction Executive

`http://jobs.constructionexecutive.com`

This is a job site for executives in the architecture, construction, and engineering industries, as well as related manufacturing industries (steel, piping, wire, and other building products, and heavy equipment, for example).

ExecuNet $$

`www.execunet.com`

Well rated, but as with all such things on the Net and off, research carefully why this particular service or site is different, better, and necessary before you plunk down that credit card. Memberships start at $150 for ninety days.

INTERNATIONAL

Best Jobs

`www.bestjobsus.com`

This is the U.S. site in a series of sites with job postings from various countries. The database is not the most extensive, but it's not an area where extensive listings are often found. The jobs that are here are searchable and browsable (nice feature) by location, industry, and how recent the listing is. Many jobs are shared among the various sites, and listed as "overseas."

The site does have a lot to recommend it. I particularly like the data on the employers in the database, which lets you look at individual employers in a variety of ways; see how many employers are in which cities and states; and see how many positions each employer has listed on the site.

Here are the websites for the other countries in the network:

Australia	www.bestjobsau.com
Canada	www.bestjobsca.com
Ireland	www.bestjobsie.com
New Zealand	www.bestjobs.co.nz
South Africa	www.bestjobsza.com
United Kingdom	www.bestjobsuk.com
Singapore	www.bestjobssg.com
India	www.bestjobsindia.com
Malaysia	www.bestjobsmy.com
Philippines	www.bestjobsph.com
Kenya	www.bestjobske.com
Indonesia	www.bestjobsid.com
Hong Kong	www.bestjobshk.com

Workopolis
www.workopolis.com/index.html

This is a Canadian job site that is partnered with (and its ownership situation is very similar to) CareerBuilder here in the States. I would wager it has similar benefits and liabilities. There are better-than-average resources for the job-hunter, including Bob Rosner's *Working Wounded* column. If you are looking for a Canadian job, this might be a good place to start.

Jobsite
www.jobsite.co.uk/home/advsearch.html

A United Kingdom site with jobs in the U.K. (of course), Europe, and the Middle East. Not necessarily a lot in every country—as few as thirteen vacancies listed, for some, when I visited.

Eurojobs
www.eurojobs.com

Has listings for jobs in a surprising number of countries; you can search by standard keywords and location or browse jobs by country. Currently not as large a database as one might hope.

Australia's Careers OnLine
www.careersonline.com.au/menu.html

A pretty good job board, regardless of the area it serves. The jobs database is for Australian jobs, of course, but there's a good, if slightly small, collection of resources here for everyone. I particularly like the Job Seeker's Workshop, which is a map for on-line job-hunting.

LINKS TO JOB BOARDS

There are thousands of job boards that I haven't listed. To find them, try going to these pages to see what else is available:

The 4Jobs Network
www.4jobs.com/MKT/Content/Network.asp

As mentioned earlier, 4Jobs serves as the core for hundreds—maybe even more than a thousand—job sites. Many of these are niche or international sites, and the databases can vary from one to another, even though a lot of the listed jobs will be common to all. At any rate, this page contains a list of, and links to, all of the sites that are part of the 4Jobs network. It's an impressive list.

Top 100 Job Boards
www.interbiznet.com/ern/archives/
030813.html

Well, at least in 2003, according to the Alexa rankings.

Academic360.com
`www.academic360.com`

> Links to many resources for those seeking a job in academia. Good site.

Open Directory Project
`http://dmoz.org/Business/`
`Employment/Job_Search`

> From the Open Directory Project, this is a directory of career sites on the Internet. If you are looking for a niche site that may be somewhat obscure, this directory is likely to have it.

Jobs for the Disabled at Careers.Org
`www.careers.org/topic/01_jobs_55.html`

> A *very* good list of links for job-hunters with disabilities.

Usenet
`www.jobbankusa.com/newsgrou.html`

> I don't think that there is much future in using Usenet for disseminating job openings, and I don't think you should *ever* post your resume this way. But if you want to cover all bases, here is a list of job-listing newsgroups. You can count on almost any jobs found this way to be IT oriented, academic, or extremely specialized.

FOR-FEE RESUME SERVICES

ResumeBlaster $$
`www.resumeblaster.com`

> Resume posting job banks existed long before the Internet came along, and their history has always been the same: fee or free are equally long shots for finding a job. Putting them online changes nothing.
>
> This well-known for-fee resume site has various levels of service, starting at $49 and going up from there. For the basic fee, your

resume is sent to three thousand or more recruiters and industry employers. For an extra $20, all personal information in your resume is suppressed, and you are given an anonymous email address at the ResumeBlaster site, to which any recruiter interested in you must reply. Unless you respond to that recruiter, your identity is never known. Other services are available for various prices.

VOLUNTEERING

There are a number of reasons to volunteer:

- It can be a route toward a paid position at an organization, where you can demonstrate your skills and value to the organization without straining its limited payroll resources.

- It can be a good thing to do if you are currently unemployed or waiting for a new job to start, and you have time on your hands that you don't need to spend job-hunting. Helping others is much better, karma-wise, than watching Jerry Springer.

- Since networking is the quickest route to a new job, this is one more way to increase the number and range of people that you know, who may be able to help you find work.

If volunteering seems like something you would like to do, whatever your reasons, then here are some sites to try:

VolunteerMatch
`www.volunteermatch.org`

A good site for finding programs in your area. Mentoring, community projects, outreach to the elderly, local library book drives, neighborhood food banks . . . the list is endless. It even has a Virtual Volunteer section, where you can, for instance, donate your time to animal rights, conservation, and philanthropic organizations that need Web designers, grant writers, artists, and so on. A *very* good site.

ServeNet
`www.servenet.org`

Another volunteer site, also with quite a few listings. This site is somewhat more polished than VolunteerMatch; it has resources

on the site, like tip sheets for volunteers, articles about volunteering, news clips, and the current temperature, which is always important to know whenever you get the urge to help somebody. The site has a lot to recommend it, including sections on virtual volunteering, a listing of jobs for pay currently open at nonprofits and social-conscience organizations, newsletters you can sign up for . . . there's quite a bit here.

Volunteer Canada
`www.volunteer.ca/index-eng.php`

This is a government-funded website for volunteering in Canada. It's more of a clearinghouse for information than an actual place to look for situations. To volunteer, you link up with one of the two hundred volunteer centers (well, okay, *centres*) across Canada at `www.volunteer.ca/volcan/eng/content/ vol-centres/locations.php?display=1,0,6`.

Global Volunteer Network
`www.volunteer.org.nz/programs`

This site, also, is more of an information clearinghouse for various programs around the world than a site for placing volunteers in such programs. Accent is on overseas programs in depressed areas.

WorldVolunteerWeb.org
`www.worldvolunteerweb.org`

This is the site created by the United Nations to serve as a center for information, organizations, and programs related to volunteering on a global basis. This site is best for getting a worldview of volunteering in general; if you are looking for hands-on situations, then the other sites listed here are more likely to be useful to you.

POSTSCRIPT

If all of the time you spend on the job boards pays off for you, and you get the job you most desire, great! But if not, just remember that job boards are the face of the Internet that is, statistically, the least effective for job-hunting. Don't let any lack of success on the boards depress you; it's just the same old Neanderthal job-hunting system our country loves and knows so well, albeit in a new dress.

Rather, redouble your efforts to follow the themes of *Parachute*, and use the Net in the ways it is most effective.

The Internet

CHAPTER SIX

A Beginner's Primer on the Internet

If you're a beginner with the Internet, and you want to understand it better, it might be helpful to look at a little history first.

THE HISTORY

We may define the last three or four decades, computer-wise, in broad terms. The '60s and '70s can be thought of as the Era of the Mainframe Computer. It was originally a huge thing, which could fill a whole room. Hooked up to it were terminals, smaller machines that were used to run programs on the mainframe. These smaller machines lacked any permanent data storage of their own; hard drives and other storage mediums were too expensive, and were reserved for use only by mainframes. The mainframe acted as what would later be called a *server*—a machine that provides services to other computers.

With the 1980s, we moved into a new era: the Era of the Desktop Computer. Apple, the TRS-80, and the Pet and Commodore computers became available, and with IBM's introduction of the PC in 1984, the personal computer was firmly established. These computers were self-contained, and had their own data-storage systems (originally, floppy disks, eventually hard drives). By the end of the decade, these computers were nearly the equal of some of the older mainframes, in terms of computing power, storage, and speed.

With the coming of the '90s, we moved into still another era, which may be thought of as the Era of the Network. Computers spend most of their time waiting for the next command from their human operators; this was not a very efficient use of such expensive machines. But people found that by hooking up cheaper, slower computers to the faster, more expensive ones, the fast ones could operate as servers for the cheaper ones, the *clients*. The resultant *networks* were a far more efficient use of computing resources and dollars. Eventually, as the personal computers became more powerful, networks were made of many types of computers, so they could all share data and resources such as storage devices and printers. The networks expanded.

As prices of computers and storage devices dropped and computing power rose, technology was developed to hook networks to networks; servers for one network could serve other networks as well; client computers could reach out for information from any of the other networks they were hooked up to. As more networks hooked to more networks, the inter-network, or *Internet*, was born.

From the mid-90s through the present day, with the birth of the World Wide Web and the commercialization of the Internet, more and more servers are constantly being added to service the increasing number of clients. Every person who connects to the Internet increases the size, power, and reach of this huge, global network.

THE WORLD WIDE WEB

Networked—and inter-networked—computers communicate with each other using a variety of *protocols*—essentially, agreements on the form of the communications between machines. These protocols have various names: listserv, ftp, mailserv, and so on. In 1990, Tim Berners-Lee, at CERN, the European Particle Physics Laboratory in Geneva, Switzerland, thought of applying a technology called *hypertext* to create another protocol for networked computers. This hypertext transfer protocol led to the birth of a new addition to the Internet, the World Wide Web.

Hyper Text Transfer Protocol, or http, embeds the address of another computer, or computer file, into words or graphics referred to as *hyperlinks*. Clicking on a hyperlink can transport you to a different computer site, or different file, among networked computers, anywhere on the network. With the Internet, that means anywhere in the world. You need only mouse-click on the designated word, series of words, or graphic on your screen that has the embedded hyperlink. The location of the serving computer, the physical location of the hyperlink-connected file, is completely invisible and irrelevant to the user.

The World Wide Web came along at the same time that increased graphics capabilities were becoming available for personal computers. Now, you could see more than just the printed word on the screen; graphics, charts, and visuals could burst from your computer monitor, and they, in turn, could serve as hyperlinks to other data, graphics, and sound. Even plain old text could be all gussied up, in colors and various fonts, so that it looked interesting and attractive. With the Web, the Internet had acquired a new face—interface, that is—and a new makeup. It had color. It had pictures. It looked wonderful. Moreover, you could create your own website and Web page, if you wished, and there display whatever you wanted to. It was, and is, democracy in action.

With this invention of the Web interface, computers and the Internet became interesting to the population at large. People perked up. The Internet started attracting the masses. Even if you didn't have access to a computer at work, a desktop computer at home could give you Internet access with just a modem, a telephone line, and an Internet service provider (ISP) who, for a fee, would give you access to, and make your computer a part of, the Internet.

ADDRESSES ON THE INTERNET: URLS

How does it work, once you're "on the Internet"? Well, displayed on your computer screen should be your *browser:* Netscape Navigator or Microsoft Internet Explorer, in all likelihood. If there's some site you want to go to—you saw it mentioned somewhere, and you know the electronic address of that site, sometimes called its Location or Uniform Resource Locator (URL)—all you have to do is type the URL (carefully) into the window toward the top of your browser (or use the Open Location command), press the Enter key on your computer, and—almost magically—your browser will take you to that site.

The URL is a unique address: it leads directly to *that* particular website, wherever it is in the world, and to the *exact* file you seek. You will have noticed that every company or organization is now putting its web address, or URL, at the bottom of its newspaper or TV ad. You've probably seen it written like:

    www.google.com

(Or it may say, "We're on the Web at `google dot com`.")

Actually, though, the computers involved need to know more than just the address; they have to agree on the protocol, or language, by which they will communicate. For the Web, the default protocol is http, which is why your Web browser will automatically add the protocol to the address so that it reads:

    http://www.google.com

This means, "Using *hyper*text *t*ransfer *p*rotocol, connect me to a computer on the World Wide Web named *google*, which is, by the way, a *com*mercial venture." The "google.com" address is then converted into a number, like "206.232.128.2," which the Internet's internal workings use to find the actual computer that contains the data you want.

You can go to still other computers and Web pages by typing in their respective URLs or, more efficiently for you, by just clicking on *hyperlinks,* or links in the page currently displayed in your browser. Hyper-clicking will load a new page's URL into the browser automatically, and you are then transported to the new page, as if by magic.

WEBSITES

A website is usually not a single page, but a group of pages. Likewise, the URLs that specify these pages and page groups are hierarchical: they go from general to specific as you move from left to right. Take an example from the Job-Hunter's Bible website: there is an article on the site called, "The Three Dangers of Resumes." Here is the URL for that article:

```
http://www.jobhuntersbible.com/
library/hunters/threedangers.shtml
```

Broken down, the first part, "`http://`", just says that the computers involved—yours as the client, the other as the server—are going to communicate in hypertext transfer protocol. The next part, "`www.jobhuntersbible.com`," says that we are looking for a computer on the Web named "JobHuntersBible .com." The next part, "`library`," says to take us to a section on the JHB site called "library." See—we're getting more specific as we go. Next, "`hunters`" says to take us to the library section for job-hunters, and "`threedangers.shtml`" points us to the actual document in that section of the library, named "threedangers," which is written in secure hypertext markup language.

There are probably more parts to the library than just the section for job-hunters; it's likely that there are more sections at Job-Hunter's Bible than just the library. Sometimes, by editing the URL in your browser's address window, you can go exploring around a website to see what's there. If you get a "page not found" error—a common occurrence, considering the rapid change occurring every day on the Web—a standard technique is to edit the URL, successively chopping off the more specific terms on the right of the URL and pressing the Enter key, until a legitimate page is found (or there is no more URL left!).

SEARCH ENGINES AND DIRECTORIES

The Internet is *big*. It is so big that no one knows how big it is, and they certainly don't know how to find everything on it. There is no index, or table of contents, and if there were, it would be useless because the contents of the Net are changing every day, every minute. The closest we can get to an index is to use a *search engine*.

Search engines are discussed in more detail in chapter 2, but essentially, a search engine is a computer program that crawls around to whatever pages it can find on the Web. As it crawls, it builds an index of certain words, and remembers the pages where it found those words. Then, when you type in a search term, the engine looks in its index for matching words and displays summaries of the appropriate Web pages. You can then click on any that look interesting and be transported to those pages through hypertext.

What kind of keywords do you type in? Think about what you are looking for, and try to think of the single word, or fewest words, that could describe Web pages useful to your inquiry. You might type in words such as "Jobs AND Seattle," if that were your interest. Or "career advice," "recipes," "auto sales," "Abraham Lincoln," "social careers," or whatever—anything about which you're looking for more information. Each search engine is a little different, and each has a page on its website that will tell you more about how to use it most effectively.

LEARNING MORE ABOUT THE NET

If you want to know more about the Internet, and you know enough to at least get connected, here are some websites where you can go to learn more:

Learn the Internet
`www.aarp.org/learninternet`

From the good folks at AARP, the best tutorial for beginners I have found.

Learn Basic Browsing
`www.aarp.org/learninternet/basic_browsing`

Also from AARP, very helpful for the novice.

Beginner's Central
`www.northernwebs.com/bc`

A bit old—it was written in 1998—yet just about the most thorough Internet manual around.

Sources

INTRODUCTION

. . . your chances of finding a job are less than 10 percent:
U.S. Department of Labor, Bureau of Labor Statistics
`www.bls.gov/home.htm`.

CHAPTER ONE

Net usage statistics: `www.internetworldstats.com` and
particularly `www.internetworldstats.com/stats2`
`.htm`—their sources include Nielson/NetStats and ITC.

17 million people logged on to career sites on the Internet:
Nielson/Net Ratings, `www.nielsen-netratings`
`.com/pr/pr_030516.pdf`.

Net use, job-hunt statistics: Pew Internet and American Life Project:
`www.pewinternet.org`. Article about: `www.clickz.com/`
`stats/markets/professional/article.php/1437221`;
see also U.S. Department of Labor, Bureau of Labor Statistics,
`www.bls.gov/home.htm`.

Usenet as part of the Net: Technically, Usenet is not part *of* the Net
but is accessible *through* the Net. Practically speaking, there is no
difference.

DHMO: *Scientific American,* June 2004, page 113; see also
`www.dhmo.org`.

4 percent of Net job-hunters: "The Career Networks," *Forrester
Research,* Spring 2000.

8 percent of new hires: Employment Management Association's 2000
"Cost Per Hire and Staffing Metrics Survey," as reported in *Weddle's*
8/1/00.

3 percent more likely, then 3 percent less likely: "Online Job Applications Less Effective: Study," CNETAsia, `asia.cnet.com/newstech/systems/0,39001153,39146166,00.htm`.

30 percent increase in traffic to Net job sites: Stockwatch.com, "U.S. Job Recovery Pushes 30 Percent Growth for Online Career Sites," 7/16/04, `http://biz.yahoo.com/prnews/040716/sff017_1.html`.

2003 study of companies that hired through the Internet: CareerXRoads study, published in its newsletter 1/31/03.

2003 study, 61 percent found jobs through contacts: Bernard Haldane Associates Internet Job Report, conducted by Taylor Nelson Sofres Intersearch, reported by Andrea Coombes, `CBS Marketwatch.com` 1/23/2003.

Supersites/Net job-hunters: Nielson/NetRatings report, June 2004, and 7/16/04 news release: "U.S. Job Recovery Pushes 30 Percent Growth for Online Career Sites," `http://biz.yahoo.com/prnews/040716/sff017_1.html`.

CHAPTER TWO

MetaXCrawler mixes sponsored results with "real" results: `www.lib.berkeley.edu/TeachingLib/Guides/Internet/MetaSearch.html`.

The five criteria for evaluating search results: `www.Widener.Edu/Wolfgram-Memorial-Library/Webevaluation/Inform.htm` and `www.Sofweb.Vic.Edu.Au/Internet/Research.htm`.

Yahoo! has own search engine; Teoma, Alta Vista, others mix paid results: `http://news.netcraft.com/archives/2004/04/23/desperately_seeking_web_search_20.html`.

CHAPTER THREE

Calling around, 69 percent and 84 percent success rates: the information comes from Azrin, Hoffman, and Curtis; see footnote on page 42 of the 2005 edition of *What Color Is Your Parachute?*

2003 study shows 60 percent of new hires through referrals and the Net: CAREERXROADS Third Annual Source of Hires Study, January 2004, Gerry Crispin and Mark Mehler, `www.careerxroads.com`.

Less than 10 percent through the Net: in chapter 1, I quoted two studies that showed that 4 percent and 8 percent of new hires were through the Net. The sources were

4 percent of Net job-hunters: "The Career Networks," *Forrester Research*, Spring 2000.

8 percent of new hires: Employment Management Association's 2000 "Cost Per Hire and Staffing Metrics Survey," as reported in *Weddle's* 8/1/00.

We each know 250 people: "The Law of 250," `www.collegegrad.com/jobsearch/8-1.shtml`.

About the Authors

Richard N. Bolles is the author of the most popular career-planning and job-hunting book in the world, *What Color Is Your Parachute? A Practical Manual for Job-Hunters and Career-Changers,* which has over eight million copies currently in print, is purchased by 20,000 people a month, and exists in twelve languages. It is updated annually. He is an alumnus of the Massachusetts Institute of Technology, in chemical engineering; Harvard University, in physics (where he graduated cum laude); and the General Theological (Episcopal) Seminary in New York City, from which he holds a master's degree in New Testament studies. He is listed in *Who's Who in America,* and *Who's Who in the World.* He lives in the San Francisco Bay Area.

Mark Emery Bolles, Dick's second son, has long served as assistant to his father and more recently as editor of *What Color Is Your Parachute?* and the previous edition of *Job-Hunting on the Internet.* He has worked as a luthier, computer programmer, musician, and technical writer.

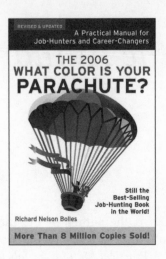

What Color Is Your Parachute?
A Practical Manual for Job-Hunters
and Career-Changers

is the best-selling job-hunting book in the world. At least 20,000 people have bought the book each month for the past thirty-five years, and there are now more than eight million copies in print.

What do readers like about the book? In thousands of letters to the author, over the years, readers have cited the following four things that they like about the book:

1. It works. It gives a step-by-step process for getting around all the obstacles normally encountered in the job-hunt, which people have successfully used to change jobs or careers, over the past three decades.

2. It is always up to date. Its annual revisions allow it to keep up with the latest job-hunting techniques, and the latest changes in the job market.

3. It takes seriously the fact that people are in a great hurry. But it also takes seriously those who wish to be more thorough, and it includes a series of practical exercises for matching yourself to a job.

4. It covers many subjects that other job-hunting books don't, such as "how to choose a career counselor," listing names of counselors, and "how to find your mission in life" for people of faith.

Index

clustering and, 42–44
definition of, 196
directories vs., 30
help pages for, 44–45
limitations of, 47, 51
meta-, 40–42
methods used by, 34–35, 42–43
non-HTML data and, 46–47, 48–49
purpose of, 33
specialized, 45–47
using, 35–37
SearchEngines.com, 46
Search Engine Watch, 37
Securities and Exchange Commission (SEC), 71
SEDAR, 71
Self-Directed Search (SDS), 138
Self-discipline, 98
Self-employment, 76–79
ServeNet, 176, 187–88
Servers, 191
Sherman, Chris, 53, 97
SHRM Jobs, 175
6FigureJobs, 182
Skills
Internet, 6
motivated, 141
transferable, 141–42
Slyck's Guide to the Newsgroups, 96
Small Business Administration (SBA), 76–77
SmartPages, 66
SnagAJob, 80, 182
Society of Research Administrators (SRA) International, 91
SofWeb, 98
Spam, 128–30
Spy programs, 128
Startup Journal, 77
State departments of education, 89
State employment offices, 147
StyleCareers, 171
Summerjobs.com, 81, 181
SuperPages, 66
Supersites, 21–28, 159, 161–64

T

Taxes, 78–79
Teachers Support Network, 177
techies.com, 173
Technical Communication Library, 52
Technical writers, 178
Telecommuting Jobs, 178
Temporary work, 80–81, 180–82
Teoma, 39, 44, 48
Tests. *See also* Career counseling
career, 135–40
personality, 131–35
transferable skills, 141
Thank-you notes, 125
Thomas Global Register, 64, 70
ThomasNet, 70
Thomas Register, 70
Threads, 107–8
Tile.Net, 49–50, 115, 116
Topica, 53, 116
Transferable skills, 141–42
Tribe, 114, 118
TrueCareers, 170–71
200 Letters for Job Hunters, 155

U

U.C. Berkeley, 51–52, 55
UnderWeb, 51–55
University at Albany, 37, 55
University career centers, 147
University of British Columbia, 73
University of Minnesota, 141
University of Missouri, 138
University of South Carolina, 37
University of Waterloo, 142, 154
University of Wisconsin, 141
URLs
avoiding laborious typing of, xii–xiii
definition of, 194–95
mining, 48
nonworking, xiv, 196
parts of, 195
U.S. Census Bureau, 59
U.S. Department of Education, 91

U.S. Department of Health and Human Services, 91
U.S. Department of Labor, 59, 86, 141, 162
U.S. Patent and Trademark Office, 54
USAJobs, 180
Usenet, 12–13, 95–97, 108–10, 186

V

Vault, 67, 124
Virginia Tech, 155
Virtual Chase, 72
Virtual Community of Associations, 64
Viruses, 128–29
Vocational Information Center, 60
Vocational tests, 135–40
Volunteer Canada, 188
Volunteering, 187–89
VolunteerMatch, 187

W

Wall Street Journal, 73, 113, 140, 143, 154, 183
Weather Channel, 57
Weddle, Peter, 127
Weddle's, 64, 123
WetFeet, 72, 102, 111, 144, 156
What Color Is Your Parachute?, ix–x, 4, 10, 20
Whois.com, 69, 123
Whois.Net, 69, 123
Will, Gary, 156
Wireless access hot spots, xii
Women, 83–85, 89, 119, 149, 179

WomensJobSearch.net, 179
Work at home schemes, 79
Working Solo, 77
WORKink, 87, 180
Workopolis, 184
Work Support, 86
WorldVolunteerWeb.org, 189
World Wide Web. *See also* Internet; URLs
definition of, 10–11
fee-for-service sites, xii
growth of, 1–2
history of, 193–94
navigating, 11, 195–96
number of job-hunting sites on, 11–12
World Wide Web Tax, 78–79
WorldWIT, 119
WWWomen, 84

Y, Z

Yahoo!
Chat, 111
Company Directories, 68, 124
Directory, 31–32
Education, 149
Finance, 72
Groups, 112
HotJobs, 21, 25, 113, 139, 161–62
Professional Organizations, 63
Search, 35, 40, 44, 49
Yale University, 130
Yellow.com, 65–66, 104
Yellow Wood, 144
ZipFind, 57

210